Why Teaching Matters

A Philosophical Guide to the Elements of Practice

Paul Farber and
Dini Metro-Roland

BLOOMSBURY ACADEMIC
LONDON · NEW YORK · OXFORD · NEW DELHI · SYDNEY

Bloomsbury Academic
An imprint of Bloomsbury Publishing Plc
50 Bedford Square, London, WC1B 3DP, UK
1385 Broadway, New York, NY 10018, USA

www.bloomsbury.com
BLOOMSBURY and the Diana logo are trademarks of Bloomsbury Publishing Plc

First published 2020

Cover design by Irene Martinez Costa
Cover image © Lera Efremova / Adobe Stock

A catalogue record for this book is available from the British Library.

A catalog record for this book is available from the Library of Congress.

Library of Congress Cataloging-in-Publication Data

ISBN: HB: 978-1-3500-9776-6
PB: 978-1-3500-9777-3
ePDF: 978-1-3500-9779-7
ePub: 978-1-3500-9778-0

Typeset by Deanta Global Publishing Services, Chennai, India
Printed and bound in Great Britain

To all the teachers who mattered and matter still

Contents

Preface

This book began with a brochure. Several years ago, we saw a flyer announcing newly begun online courses that a university was promoting—at the time, a new frontier for students to consider. Several reasons were highlighted for giving these courses a try. One was the idea that you could take a course in your pajamas. Another was the promise of an end to parking hassles on campus. Frankly we forget the others, though none made reference to the quality of teaching in question.

The courses involved a new way of teaching and being taught. We didn't know what to make of that, and the details were sketchy. What did register was a feeling. In this new initiative, teaching was being both transformed and disregarded. It was malleable but not what mattered— parking problems mattered more. In fairness, a lot of attention was probably being given to course design at that time, the issues of how to deliver instruction online. But it seemed to us that teaching itself— what it means to teach and be taught, what's involved in teaching, and the many kinds of impact teaching can have—was an afterthought. It struck us, in short, that teaching matters. But why? We decided then to give this some thought.

What was originally going to be a short conference paper turned into something of a journey. It quickly became apparent that teaching itself is a rather unruly subject matter. The terrain seems familiar enough, but such familiarity with a subject can also be deceiving. Anyone with any experience teaching or being taught will have formed some ideas about teaching. We all have views about the range of ways teachers go about their work and what the work is or might be good for. This was true of course for us as well. But as we explored the topic further, it was clear to us that we cared about teaching in ways that are often overlooked or undervalued. We were especially sensitive to the intrusive efforts of those who set out to control or direct the work of teachers in some way, without taking pains to think seriously about the kinds of meaning and value that teaching has in our lives.

The questions quickly multiplied. What are we talking about when we talk about teaching? Or more to the point, what is it one cares about when one cares about teaching? This is where you come in. After all, we begin with ideas about teaching and what it is we care about, but so do you. We have that in common as our starting place.

The book is written for two kinds of people:

- Those who teach—anything, at any level—or are thinking about doing so.
- Those with an interest in monitoring, reforming, administering, directing, critiquing, redesigning, or evaluating the work of teachers.

In other words, we write both for those on the "inside" of teaching and those "outside" looking in, those doing the work of teaching and those taking an interest in how that work is done. Regardless of your perspective, however, we assume that like us, you too have cares and concerns about teaching and an interest in better understanding the nature of teaching, what it involves, and why it matters. That is what this book sets out to explore.

Acknowledgments

In writing a book about teaching, we would first of all like to acknowledge our debt to our own teachers, and to all the practicing and aspiring teachers we have had the privilege to meet in our own teaching. These encounters made a true difference in our own lives in more ways than we can know or say.

We also would like to thank Western Michigan University for granting us sabbaticals that enabled us to begin our work in earnest and the Department of Teaching, Learning and Educational Studies for their patience as this project developed.

We couldn't have completed this book without the steady support and warm encouragement of our friends and colleagues from Western Michigan University's Center for the Humanities, the "Promise of Education" reading group, and the poetry dudes.

We have also benefited more than we can say from being part of the small but dedicated family of scholars engaged—in outposts worldwide—in the vital, often discordant, conversation that is the philosophy of education. Within that family, it would be folly to try listing names of those whose work and friendship have contributed most to this project, except that is, for our dear friend Al Neiman, whose questions remind us of what cannot be captured in a work of this kind. Being in the company of passionate scholars and teachers inspired us to write this tribute to teaching.

Special thanks go out to those generous readers who provided vital feedback on early drafts: Michelle Metro-Roland, Lisa Cronkhite-Marks, Seamus Mulryan, and Sarah Stiennon. Your insight and sound advice led us to a better understanding of our topic and helped us to express our ideas more clearly and concisely.

We are also grateful to Mark Richardson at Bloomsbury Press, whose initial interest, keen insights, and support of the project were essential to its realization. Thanks as well to the anonymous readers whose careful reviews of the proposal and manuscript provided valuable guidance along the way.

Finally, the partnership we have had in the writing of this book was, at times, rather consuming. Our families took note of this and responded with the kind of loving support we have come to expect but for which we are profoundly grateful.

In Paul's case, Laurie no doubt noticed and patiently endured the ups and downs of work on this book, but her love and support were the one constant as the work took shape, and her wholehearted devotion to the actual work of teaching, to being every day the teacher that she is, was to someone writing a book about teaching nothing short of an inspiration.

Dini is especially grateful for Michelle's continual love, affection, and understanding through it all. Not only did she contribute insightful critical assessments exactly when we needed to hear them, but she also kindly took over many of my duties as the project demanded more (and still more) of my attention. Dini also appreciates the way everyone in the house (Michelle, Elek, Éva and Liliána) laughed off his (occasional) irritable moods with the exceptional wit that he has come to expect from this family.

One further thing to note. As equal partners in the writing of this book, one problem is the potentially misleading fact that our names appear in sequence; but to be clear, all credit is equally shared. There is an advantage to co-authoring a book as well, however. We are the best of friends, but we have often scrapped like brothers. Each of us can now take comfort in the fact that any shortcomings or outright blunders that remain in this book are, without a doubt, *his* fault and not mine.

Introduction

Why *does* teaching matter? At first glance, this is not a difficult question. In fact, anyone reading this could say why they are grateful for teachers in their lives. There are personal accomplishments that key teachers helped them to attain. Many are equally grateful for the ways in which their children benefit from what good teaching provides. In vocations, professions, and practices of all kinds virtually everyone involved has teachers to whom they owe gratitude. And more broadly still, all members of healthy communities, stable nations, and thriving economies can surely identify the kinds of teaching that make such collective accomplishments possible and sustainable. Teaching is instrumental to what we value in our lives in all kinds of ways.

But where deep problems confront us in any of the domains noted above, it is not difficult to complain about what teaching has gotten wrong or failed to provide. So teaching matters, too, with respect to what we believe we should get from it but don't, at least not enough or not yet. Thinking about teaching in terms of its immediate instrumental value or outcomes seems to address everything important, good and bad, about why teaching matters.

This instrumental way of thinking about teaching is also enormously popular, sometimes productive, and often lucrative. It generates a regular tide of commentaries and perspectives on what teaching ought to provide or do a better job of bringing about. It frames the flood of research on teacher effectiveness and "what works" in teaching, aimed at enhancing the effectiveness of teaching in delivering certain results. Such thinking also stimulates efforts to administer, govern, evaluate, redirect, manage, or optimize teaching so that it might provide more of what various individuals, interest groups, business interests, or governing bodies want from the work of teachers. And on top of all that, there is the emerging promise of technological innovations to advance learning online in ways that might streamline or bypass teaching altogether in order to gain what we want from teaching in new ways—in a sense, getting the benefits of teaching without the bother of dealing with teachers at all.

There is a problem, however. This way of thinking, framed in terms of what we *get* from teaching—what it is or might be useful for—quite often eclipses our capacity to think about what teaching *is*. When this happens, we fail to comprehend what the work of teaching is all about, the range of demands it involves, and the deep impacts of many kinds that teaching in fact has on our lives. Preoccupied with results of one kind or another that we would want teaching to provide, we become blinded to what is, in all its troublesome complexity, the stubborn reality of teaching itself, and why that matters.

The Focus of This Book

This book focuses on teaching as a distinctive form of human activity. We aim to step back from the issues of the day and see the work of teachers in a different light. This involves trying to take what we, and you, know about teaching, the first hand experiences we all have had and the various ways we tend to think about teaching, and set that aside for the moment. The aim is to think about teaching in the most general sense possible and in that way, to enhance our capacity to see better what teaching is—here and now, wherever—and why it matters.

In stating our case for why teaching matters, we make two claims about teaching. The first is that teaching is an essential human endeavor—a particular form of activity that is both characteristic of and vital to human life. As language-using, cooperatively engaged social beings, teaching is bound up in our lives, and has been from the dawn of cultural evolution. Indeed, as a form of activity, teaching is the mother of human activities. Think of various kinds of human activity in which cultural groups take part in distinctive ways. All animals eat, but we invest time and energy, in all kinds of often elaborate ways, *preparing* what we eat. All animals have their useful capabilities with respect to objects they encounter in their environment, but we *fashion* things, sometimes in sophisticated, ornamental ways. All seek shelter, but we *create* and *inhabit* a home. All animals eventually die, but we *ceremoniously attend* to the bodies of the dead, to say nothing of practices concerning their spirit or soul. Whatever you think of particular practices of these, and many other kinds, it is teaching that enables such practices, and the complex traditions of practice stemming from them, to persist, evolve, and multiply across the generations.

Our second claim is that teaching, as a form of activity, is inherently problematic. This stems from the fact that teaching invariably involves acting on human interests of one kind or another, seeking to advance aims and seek ends that are contestable and often in conflict with the interests and aims of others. Competing interests often collide, and this makes teaching, especially in public settings today, inescapably political in nature, something subject to ongoing disputes and institutional controls, safeguards, directives, and compromise. But more than this, the nature of the activity of teaching itself—comprised of many elements, as we will see—is demanding, impactful, and unpredictable in ways that heighten the sense of its problematic nature. Diverse individual and societal considerations bear on what takes place and comes of it. Rarely in teaching is everyone pleased; the sources of dissatisfaction are abundant.

One other observation about teaching is worth noting at the outset. Whatever you are trying to teach, you never teach only that. In addition to being an age-old and problematic human endeavor, teaching is notoriously prone to unintended consequences. Of course, teaching is in part defined by its intentional nature; teachers can always give an answer to the question of what they are trying to bring about or achieve, the ends they are seeking. But the form of this activity is composed of many characteristic concerns and considerations, things to which teachers must attend as they pursue their intended purposes. As we shall see in the chapters that follow, the characteristic features of teaching, the elements of its practice, are all complex and contentious in their own ways. Each presents challenges and difficulties that cannot be readily avoided; all of them make demands that teachers cannot sidestep or disregard. And importantly, how each of the elements is addressed in practice and in turn combine generates effects and consequences of many kinds. From our point of view, to understand teaching by way of some set of specific, intended goals and results is to scarcely understand it at all.

Why a Philosophical Guide?

You can of course find all sorts of guidebooks on teaching. Most of them provide strategies and blueprints for tackling thorny educational problems or applying particular teaching methods or approaches. There are hundreds of books on teaching methods, classroom management, test and university preparation, and novel ways to teach reading, soccer, music, and just about anything else worth teaching about. Works such as these can be extremely valuable; the best of them enrich the profession in all sorts of ways. But our focus is broader and more inclusive.

Our hope is to provide readers with a philosophical guide to teaching, a way to think about teaching more comprehensively, setting aside for a time our various particular commitments to steer it in some direction. As a most venerable form of human activity, teaching deserves to be studied for its own sake and not strictly for some specific purpose that it serves. Take a step back and see teaching more fully for what it is, in all its complexity. Doing so does not derail one's commitments; if anything, it places them in the context of a more realistic appraisal of what teaching is and involves.

A philosophical perspective also provides some freedom to tackle the kinds of challenges involved in addressing a form of activity that is both essential and deeply problematic. It helps us to draw things together in a way that makes things comprehensible and awakens further interest in the issues and questions that we will encounter along the way. Fortunately, you won't need any philosophical expertise to use this book. Our guide is intended for the lay reader, no prior philosophical training is required. All we ask for is your willingness to explore many facets of teaching that are often overlooked, and to think in fresh ways about what comes into view and why it matters.

Before setting out, we should alert you to some of this guide's central themes. We seek to

- Study teaching for its own sake, setting aside the usual (and understandable) preoccupations with the specific kinds of outcomes and results normally associated with the work of teaching.
- Explore teaching as a form of activity in terms of the basic elements that comprise it—the characteristic features of the activity that come into play and combine wherever and whenever teaching takes place.
- Provide multiple perspectives on teaching and its many problematic features, including important philosophical concepts and theories that deserve more attention in public discussions about education today.

On What Teaching Is

How do we begin to see teaching in a more comprehensive and realistic way? The first step, already noted, is to avoid succumbing to the trap of reducing teaching to selected instrumental purposes or defining teaching so narrowly that we ignore the remarkable diversity of practice. Teaching is a deeply human form of activity that transpires in countless particular situations and settings. It is important to keep this variety in mind when seeking to comprehend what it is. Fortunately, anyone reading this book has considerable experience on the subject. That provides a starting place. We invite you to keep that experience in mind, but urge you to think about teaching in other contexts as well. The aim is to get at what teaching as a form of human activity involves, regardless of who or what is being taught, and when or where in the world it is taking place.

To get at this general account of what teaching involves, we need to step back from our own particular ideas about what teaching is good for, and set aside what you like or dislike about the examples of teaching that stand out in your thinking. The question for now is not what makes for *good* teaching, but what makes something teaching at all. Wherever teaching takes place—however varied the circumstances and the people involved—certain underlying concerns and considerations come into play. As these matters are addressed in practice, teaching transpires in the process. We call these common considerations and concerns the elements of teaching.

The Elements of Teaching

The chapters that follow take up the elements in detail, but a brief account is helpful here. For a start, think of a few teachers who are preferably very different in style or kind, and not necessarily "the best" or model teachers. We suspect that as you reflect on the work of these teachers, however admirable, ordinary, or even misguided in your view their teaching may be, you can recognize their need to address the following elements:

Teachers *convey care*. Teaching stems from a motivation to make a
   difference in the lives of those being taught; this often involves not
   only teachers caring about what, who, and how they teach but also
   what those they teach come to care about in turn.
Teachers *enact authority*. Whatever a teacher cares to achieve, she or
   he must establish and maintain some degree of control or guidance
   as to what the students are doing and learning over time.
Teachers *display* and *cultivate virtue*. In both conveying care and
   enacting authority, teachers draw upon and inevitably reveal
   something about their own qualities of mind and character that are
   bound up in who they are and what they aim to do. In doing so,
   they promote a range of such qualities in those they teach.

Teachers *interpret (and help students interpret) the subject matter.*
All teachers must make practical sense of the content of their
instruction, what the subject matter is and why they are teaching it.
At the same time, they must address how their students understand
the meaning and value of what they are encountering.

Teachers *render judgment.* Teaching involves attending to diverse
aspects of practical activity, and acting in ways that advance
the goals and purposes being pursued. This includes ongoing
judgments about and responses to student conduct, needs,
and performance that generate both immediate and long-term
consequences of many kinds.

Teachers *articulate purpose.* As teaching is an inherently forward-
looking form of activity, teachers always express a variety of
individual, institutional, educational, and societal ends that
conceivably apply in most teaching situations but must be clarified
and prioritized in practice.

Teachers *establish a sense of place.* Given the range of considerations
noted thus far, teaching involves complex interactions over space
and time. Teachers strive to create a sense of place in which their
teaching can be readily understood and applied.

Teachers *elicit engaged presence.* Finally, as teachers and students
engage with one another, their distinctive presence with and toward
one another always generates some meaning and value in its own
right, for good or ill. More importantly, the quality of engaged
presence is a product of the way that all of the elements of teaching
combine, and amplifies their impact.

We expect this sketch raises all kinds of questions and probably a few
red flags. Who is to say what teachers ought to care about, for example,
or what purposes they should serve? Indeed, no one reading this can
be indifferent to how *any* of these elements is addressed in practice;
all of them require teacher decisions that are subject to doubt, if not
scorn. And as the elements combine in the actual settings of practice,
the questions multiply.

This is why we find most accounts of teaching sorely limited. As we have noted, the well-established pattern is to narrow the focus to some aspects of the work. But teachers have no such luxury; all of the elements demand their attention and shape their efforts. In thinking about teaching, we should start there.

In the chapters that follow, we will draw out what these elements involve and why they matter in teaching. As we hope to show, every element plays its own necessary part in teaching of all kinds. Each element is in fact uniquely complex and impactful, and as we shall discover, each is also problematic in its own ways. And when the elements combine in the actual circumstances of practice, with all the variability that the particular people and social context add to the mix, there is a great deal to sort out.

There are of course familiar patterns of teaching, especially in the institutional frameworks of schooling. But even in the most familiar of settings, the experiences of teaching and being taught are remarkably varied; students sense this from class to class, while teachers, even teaching the same material in the same place, regularly note how different each group of students and eventually each teaching experience can be. Such differences suggest how complicated it is to knit the elements together in the actual situations of practice. For better or worse, it is the way that the elements appear and combine in such situated experiences that gives each setting of teaching its distinctive character.

Key Perspectives on Teaching Today

With this initial sense of what teaching in general involves, we must acknowledge that teaching always takes place in a context. Today, that context involves a number of distinct perspectives *on* teaching which shape thinking about what teaching ought to bring about, or where it seems to go awry. Such perspectives and theories are intended to bear upon, and often aim to channel and direct, how teaching plays out.

This is not surprising. Teaching is very much alive today as an essential and problematic activity and it is understandable that there is widespread interest in the subject, particularly with respect to the kinds of teaching that take place in the varieties of schooling from preschool through university. Although our aim is to achieve some degree of philosophically informed detachment—to think of teaching in itself as a form of activity—it is important to introduce and take account of some of the key perspectives on teaching, especially those bearing on the millions of teachers who work in the various institutional contexts of practice at all levels.

While exploring the elements of teaching, we will draw particular attention to the following points of view about teaching today:

Management-driven perspectives: administrative concerns about teaching as a kind of work to be managed in the interests of maximizing certain kinds of outcomes.

Freedom-driven perspectives: liberal and libertarian concerns about the impact of teachers on the prospects for individual autonomy.

Economy-driven perspectives: concerns about teaching centering on notions and theories of human capital that regard teaching in terms of preparation for participation in the global economy.

Social justice-driven perspectives: concerns about teaching, often associated with forms of critical theory and multiculturalism, focusing upon structures of power and inequality, and the prospects of emancipation from the many forms of discrimination and oppression.

Religious-spiritual perspectives: views about teaching that are concerned with the advance of various metaphysical claims and purposes.

Post-teaching perspectives: technologically minded efforts to solve the problematic limitations and complexities of teaching by way of new forms of instructional activity designed to supplant or replace teaching as we know it.

We have views on all of these, an affinity with some. But the point of this book is not to argue for our position. From the point of view of this book, all of these perspectives strive to advance instrumental views of teaching—stake positions as to what teaching is good for. It is important to take these positions into consideration, while also acknowledging that as a venerable form of human activity, teaching predates and will likely outlast them all. Where teaching is concerned, seeing it for what it is does not preclude the relevance of external perspectives, but it calls attention to what it is that the perspectives are attempting to influence and perhaps redirect. In other words, in debating about what teachers *ought* to do, let's not lose sight of the reality of the work itself, its inherent complexity, and the distinctive and elemental demands of practice. In any event, anyone striving to influence the work of teachers, if they are to have the impact they desire, needs to understand what that work truly involves.

Finally, a further contribution we hope this book will make is to introduce selected philosophical approaches and concepts that we believe have been neglected in public discourse on education. You will notice that each chapter gives significant space to the work of one or two philosophers. This is no survey of philosophy related to education, nor is it a detailed discussion of these selected works. Rather, our aim is to suggest the ongoing pertinence of philosophical perspectives on teaching, and to provide some threads that readers may wish to pursue further.

Getting Started

You may be thinking, wait, we all have thousands of hours of experience teaching and being taught; what is left to understand? Don't be beguiled by the apparent familiarity of teaching; it is a most remarkable thing to contemplate not only for what it brings about in the world—for good or ill—but in its own right as a distinctive kind of human activity.

Teaching is typically both a humble and humbling endeavor. This book is humble in itself; it is no guide to what teachers *should* do, or how best they can do it—those are subjects for another day, subjects in fact for every day where the work of teachers is concerned. Guides are intended to assist you in exploring something in fresh ways, not to take the place of going there yourself. We hope to encourage your thinking about teaching, not convince you that we know best.

While this book cannot provide a prescription for how best to teach, it does in the end yield several insights about the value of teaching. These require time and effort that, we suspect, some will be reluctant to give to the topic of teaching. We all learn at some point, after all, to leave our teachers behind so as to get on with our lives. But that is an inclination that is worth resisting. For in striving to better understand the diverse experiences of teaching and being taught, we cannot avoid thinking about the meaning and impact of such experiences in our lives, and the ways in which teaching matters to us all.

1

Conveying Care

In Iris Murdoch's *Sandcastle,* Mor is teaching a lesson about virtue in an adult education program. He begins by addressing a comment made by one of the students:

> "Freedom," he said, "is not exactly what I would call a virtue. Freedom might be called a benefit or a sort of grace—though of course to seek it or to gain it might be a proof of merit."
>
> The greengrocer who had made the remark that surely freedom was the chief virtue, and wasn't it thinking so that differentiated us from the Middle Ages? stared intently at Mor as if drinking in his words. Mor thought, he is not really listening, he does not want to hear what I say, he knows what he thinks and is not going to reorganize his views. The words I am uttering are not the words for him.
>
> He felt again that sad guilty feeling which he had whenever he caught himself going through the motions of being a teacher without really caring to make his pupils understand. How well he knew that many teachers, including some who got high reputations from doing so, contented themselves with putting up a show, often a brilliant one, in front of those who were to be instructed—and of this performance both sides might be the dupes. Whereas the real teacher cares only for one thing, that the matter should be understood; and into that process he vanishes . . .
>
> "I'm sorry, Mr. Staveley," said Mor, "I've said nothing to the purpose. Let me try again. You say surely freedom is a virtue—and I hesitate to accept this phrase. Let me explain why. To begin with . . . freedom needs to be defined. If by freedom we mean absence of external constraint, then we may call a man lucky for being free—but why should we call him good?"

"This is the condition of virtue, and to strive for it is a virtue. But it is not itself a virtue. To call mere absence of restraint or mere kicking over the traces and flouting of conventions a virtue is to be simply romantic."

"Well, what's wrong with being romantic?" said Mr. Staveley obstinately. "Let's have 'romantic' defined, since you're so keen on definitions."

I've failed again, thought Mor, with the feeling of one who has brought the horse round the field a second time only for it to shy once more at the jump. He felt very tired and the words did not come easily. But he was prepared to go on trying.

Iris Murdoch, *The Sandcastle*[1]

To those who teach, this classroom scene is unexceptional. We have all experienced the sense of frustration, incompleteness, and impending failure evident in Mor's exchange with his adult students. Caught in a conflict of motives, teachers must decide what matters and how far one is prepared to go on trying in the face of a seemingly lost cause. The pressure to put up a show and keep students in their seats is a persistent feature of today's classrooms. It is tempting, sometimes irresistibly so, to simply go through the motions, treating teaching like any other job. And yet Mor is not alone in his dogged resolve to push forward until the matter is understood; for him this is what teaching requires, "vanishing in the process" even if it likely means "bringing the horse round" yet another time.

Whether a "real teacher cares only for one thing" is another question entirely. Mor's intentions are far from simple. He not only attends to the subject matter which he persists in trying to openly explore but he also shows concern for the students themselves, even the obstinate Mr. Staveley. Mor probably also feels some responsibility to the civic purpose of this occasion and to what he believes are his obligations as a teacher. What motivates these adult students is no doubt complex as well. Murdoch wisely leaves this to her readers' imagination, but it is clear that Mr. Staveley's prickly remarks put Mor to the test. Like

---

[1]   Iris Murdoch, *The Sandcastle* (New York: Penguin, 1978), 53–55.

teachers everywhere, Mor must prudently but forcefully meet this challenge and defend his commitments as if his authority as a teacher, and the values he represents, depend upon it. His students will surely notice if he gives up the fight.

Care is fundamentally a disposition to attend to something; to care for or about something involves the giving of attention. Iris Murdoch describes this elsewhere as "a just and loving gaze directed upon an individual reality."[2] When we attend to something outside of ourselves, we are responsive to its qualities, interests, and demands. Teachers convey care by acting on their varied pedagogical commitments in explicit ways. A teacher's care directs the attention of others; it invites active engagement and creates and strengthens mutual concern. One might even say that teaching matters to the extent that teachers care, care about what they teach, whom they teach, and why they go on teaching in spite of it all.

In this chapter, we are primarily interested in how the cares of teachers motivate and shape the educational experience. We begin with the notion of care as a disposition to attend, and consider the kinds of things that teachers tend to care about. Teachers, we argue, often convey their care with sharing intent—they invite students to participate in their commitments. Why the diverse cares of teachers matter is then put in the context of how their work, motivated by those cares, affects their students and can impact the course of their lives. We end the chapter by raising some unsettling questions about the ethics of teacher attention as their cares play out in the lives of those they teach.

The Elusive Object of Care

What does it mean when a student says that her teacher really cares? It may be that what she is actually saying is, "This teacher cares about

[2] Iris Murdoch, *Sovereignty of Good* (Boston: Ark Paperbooks, 1970), 34.

me." But that's probably not the end of it. Few students can respect a teacher who couldn't care less about what or how she teaches. And while teachers often do care in certain respects about their students, that is rarely the whole story. Teachers also care about the conditions and context of their work and their standing as teachers. And, of course, they cannot avoid caring in any number of ways about what they teach. But what does it mean *to care*?

A prominent view has been offered by Harry Frankfurt. He suggests that the mark of caring about something is the sense of pain or loss one would feel in having to give it up, turn away, or let it go. In the case of one's deepest and most enduring cares, the object of care is something to which one feels willingly committed; in that state, we desire its continued existence and we are moved to identify with and act in its best interests. For Frankfurt, the objects of such care can be many kinds of things—for example, one's child, a pet, a particular person or people, some activity or practice, certain objects in the world or abstract ideals, say truth or justice.[3] In caring about any of these things, or anything at all, it matters that they exist, and we desire what is in their interest in continuing to exist, and if possible, to do well or flourish. Because of this, the object of your care motivates your sustained attention and makes you mindful of other things in the world that are important to you, precisely because they bear on the interests of what you care about.

That determination is strengthened by another key feature of care. Frankfurt reminds us that human beings are by nature reflexive beings. This matters greatly where care is concerned. As he puts it, "Caring manifests and depends upon our distinctive capacity to have thoughts, desires, and attitudes that are *about* our own attitudes, desires, and thoughts."[4] Simply put, we care about our cares, which lends shape to our identity. Affirming that "this is what I care about" deepens the sense that "this is who I am," and vice versa. Recall Mor's frustration whenever

---

[3]   Harry Frankfurt, *The Reasons of Love* (New York: Princeton University Press, 2006), 41.

[4]   Frankfurt, *The Reasons of Love*, 17.

he finds himself caring more about putting up a show than making the subject matter understood, which for him is what truly matters in teaching. It would seem that it is his second-order conviction that he not only cares about the matter being understood but also that he *should* care, that drives him to go on trying. That is who he *is* as a teacher.

Teachers are not all cast in the same mold, however. Teachers can care about many things. First, there is the job itself. Many consider teaching to be an attractive kind of work, providing plenty of the benefits one can reasonably hope for in a job—for example, that the work is stable, that the conditions are appealing, and in the case of teaching, that it is personally meaningful and fulfilling. For those whose object of care is the job itself, it becomes a matter of genuine importance to them that they do the job well, fulfilling the terms of employment and meeting the prevailing professional and institutional expectations for this kind of work. Matters of importance arise from this kind of care. Teachers need to develop reliable expertise in doing the work, negotiate and monitor the terms and conditions set out by their administrators or employers. Teachers want to get paid of course. They also desire recognition for the work they do and often wish for greater influence over the direction of their profession. There is nothing especially demeaning or surprising about this; these same practical concerns motivate members of every profession.

Caring about the job may be a start, but when looking for the object of care in teaching, it is sorely limited. Cares also emerge from the specific nature of teaching itself. Even teachers who care exclusively about the job recognize that they must concern themselves with *whom* and *what* they teach—matters of clear importance to the teaching profession. Given the nature of the practice, it should come as no surprise that the central objects of care for many teachers are students, the subject matter, or the ways in which the two interact in practice. They have reason to care about the job, too, but it is not the principal focus of their care.

We all expect teachers to attend to their students in some way. At a minimum, we hope that they will pay heed to their students' grasp of a specific domain of knowledge and skills. An effective chemistry teacher will likely work hard to provide her students with a foundation of scientific principles and practices. She displays care for students by meticulously developing in them a familiarity with lab equipment and their usage, certain powers of observation, organization, and measurement, and knowledge of the elements and the various effects of different combinations and conditions. Of course, she can care for her students in other ways as well. She might take a keen interest in their personal lives, or work to bring out other qualities in them not directly related to science. She can do these things simply because they are pedagogically effective—that is, because building relationships promotes better student engagement—or because she is genuinely interested in their lives beyond the classroom, or some combination of the two.

Nel Noddings, a renowned scholar of care, envisions a more prominent caring role for teachers.[5] She is less interested in care as an individual attribute—such as whether one possesses a caring personality—than she is in understanding and promoting *caring relations* between individuals.[6] For Noddings, genuine care takes place as a particular form of interaction between the carer and the cared-for. Both parties have a role to play in realizing the relation. The carer must attend to the person in need with what she characterizes as *engrossment* and *motivational displacement*.[7] That is, the carer should be prepared to become fully receptive to the cared-for, and establish what is required of her at that moment (engrossment). Setting aside her own projects and designs, the carer must then align her actions with goals that are relevant and beneficial to the cared-for (motivational displacement). This can be as simple as reminding a student to write his name on his paper this time, or as drastic as scrapping an entire lesson to help students cope with a sudden tragedy. We convey care by counseling a student to give up his earlier goal of becoming a writer when that is

---

[5] Nel Noddings, *Caring: A Relational Approach to Ethics and Moral Education* (Los Angeles: California, 2013 [1984]).

[6] Noddings, *Caring*, 10–21.

[7] Noddings, *Caring*, 10–21.

the right thing for him to do as well as by allowing a conversation to wander into uncharted territory if that is where the students' interests lead.

To complete the caring relation, the person cared for must acknowledge the gesture of care. Absent such recognition the caring relation is liable to break down. Few situations are more deflating to teachers than when their best efforts are met with cold indifference. Recognition here would require at least a modicum of responsiveness to what is being taught, otherwise the teacher might succumb to apathy, the opposite of care.

Noddings believes that schooling provides ideal sites for the enactment and strengthening of caring relations. By demonstrating care for students this way, teachers create open spaces for inquiry that build on students' natural interests and encourage them to discover and exercise their unique talents, pursue their chosen goals, and show appreciation for caring and being cared for in and outside the classroom. However, current trends in schooling are mostly incompatible with this vision. Adopting Noddings' particular form of caring as a guiding principle of teaching would require a significant shift away from standardized curricula, pseudo dialogues (where the teacher knows the conclusion before the conversation begins), and other heavy-handed pedagogical strategies utilized by teachers to leverage student energies and attention toward predetermined ends. The boundaries separating school from community would also have to become more porous and formal teaching more reflective of the kind of interactions that take place organically between those who possess knowledge and skills and those who genuinely desire to acquire them.

There are other ways to care about students, however. Some approaches to teaching entail widening the horizon of what students care about beyond their immediate concerns. Sensitivity to student interests is thereby balanced by a teacher's disposition to attend to matters far apart from the present lives of students, things of the world to which the teacher is committed, such as the worthwhile qualities and ideals of a particular discipline. Teachers who care about their subject matter can only compromise so much in making it more accessible or interesting to students before the integrity of the subject matter breaks down. In fact, a student's immediate interests are often largely irrelevant when teachers see students mainly in relation to the collective tasks laid out before them. Even if teachers take time to learn and care about each student, often their primary focus is to call students' attention to the vital features of the subject matter. Whether that is applying the pick-and-roll on a basketball court or correctly solving equations for velocity and acceleration, caring for students is entangled with something larger than the students' narrow sphere of experience: it requires that students develop new abilities, new understandings, and new interests if they are to become more fully engaged in the outside world. In this respect, Mor doesn't try to satisfy Mr. Staveley's immediate interests or even to understand the reasons why he is so intent on being right. He needs to be tactful, to be sure, but only with an eye toward leading Mr. Staveley and the others to a deeper understanding of the topic at hand. Attending to students in this way takes us away from the care relations envisioned by Noddings.

This perspective also illustrates a distinctive feature of teacher care, its *sharing intent*. Teaching isn't a private affair where one jealously guards the object of one's concern from others. On the contrary, teachers convey care so that students will come to share certain commitments. At a basic level, what teachers care about directs the attention of others: "Look here. This is what matters now." It is not enough that students merely go through the motions, teachers also hope that they will treat the subject matter with respect and give it their full attention.

A sharing intent is unproblematic in certain teaching situations, especially when students are willingly there to learn a particular subject matter, such as in an elective class on cooking or on nineteenth-century literature. In such cases, the students will often scrupulously follow the teacher's directions, trusting her expertise and advice. When both parties attend to the same object of care, what primarily matters is the quality of the teacher's guidance with respect to what is relevant and important and the students' ability to apply what they learn. As students acquire and utilize new knowledge and skills, such as mastering a particular cooking technique or deriving deeper meaning from certain passages in the text, their care for the subject matter, and the bond between teacher and students, is often strengthened. The sharing intent translates as the genuinely mutual commitment of all present.

Rarely is it as simple as that. The tension between Noddings' approach to caring and those more invested in imparting particular domains of knowledge and skills is most palpable when teacher and student do not care about the same things, or in the way that teachers would hope. Sometimes students do not care about *anything* the teacher has to say to them. The most formidable challenge facing many teachers is how best to instill in students some care about what they are doing. Confronted with indifferent students, teachers must choose what to prioritize: the students' expressed or implied interests (if these can even be established), the integrity of the subject matter being taught, the learning objectives handed down from above, or something else entirely.

That apathy is a persistent problem, and not just with students but with teachers as well, might have something to do with the nature of caring itself. Caring makes one vulnerable to all sorts of frustrations. For one thing, whether the object of care is a person, idea, or thing, the carer must relinquish some control in the process of caring. Recall the way in which engrossment and motivational displacement shift power from the interests and projects of the carer to the interests and projects of the cared-for.[8] This plays out in all acts of genuine care. Frankfurt argues that the mark of genuine care, and especially of love, which for him is the deepest form of care, is showing *disinterested concern* for the well-being of what one cares about.[9] What he means by disinterested concern is really a heightened form of attention; we must try to see something for what it really is and what is in its best interests, not for what one wishes it to be or hopes to get from it.

---

[8] Noddings, *Caring*, 10–21.
[9] Frankfurt, *The Reasons of Love*, 41, 82.

That clearly applies, say, to caring for one's children, but it applies to all kinds of things one finds oneself caring about and hoping therefore to better understand. Consider your own experience tackling a particularly thorny problem in some domain of science, or reading an initially befuddling scholarly text. Assuming that you care to understand the matter in question, you must set aside your prior commitments or prevailing notions of what is true or what you wish to find. That is, you must relinquish some control and resist the temptation to dominate the subject matter with your own settled ideas. Only in that way can you begin to do justice to what is before you and why it matters. Murdoch illustrates this form of attention in acquiring a new language:

> If I am learning, for instance, Russian, I am confronted by an authoritative structure which commands my respect. The task is difficult and the goal is distant and perhaps never entirely attainable. My work is a progressive revelation of something which exists independently of me. Attention is regarded by a knowledge of reality. Love of Russian leads me away from myself towards something alien to me, something which my consciousness cannot take over, swallow up, deny or make unreal. The honesty and humility required of the student—not to pretend to know what one does not know—is the preparation of the honesty and humility of the scholar who does not even feel tempted to suppress the fact which damns his theory.[10]

The mark of genuine care, then, is the recognition of something beyond oneself that matters enough to risk coming under its influence. In fact, we become vulnerable to the object of care not only in terms of loss of control but also in the ways it can transform us as we identify with it and what is in its interests.

This poses a challenge for teachers. When addressing subject matter they care about, they must invite students to set their "just and loving gaze" upon something apart from themselves, "an individual reality,"

---

[10] Murdoch, *Sovereignty of Good*, 89.

in ways that would change them, hopefully for the better. Success is partly dependent on whether students accept the invitation. Those who have witnessed students struggle to read something challenging, or to work through a complex problem, know how humbling and precarious it can be to wholeheartedly commit to doing so, and how transformative it is when one's attention is rewarded with a new understanding or appreciation. Of course, the more we care, the greater the disappointment when our efforts come to nothing. There are many students who are not willing to take the risk of caring.

The same is true of teachers of course. Students aren't the only ones who can muddle through the day by feigning care for others and for what is being taught. Consider how many frustrations Mor might have avoided had he not cared so deeply about getting the matter understood and instead merely put on the show his audience wanted. Teachers are often caught in an entanglement of cares. In fact, the intersection between students, the subject matter, and the particular demands of the job adds a tragic element to teaching. One can't possibly care about all these things with sustained attention and intensity. Just as you succeed in convincing students to care about something worthwhile, another group comes along or the subject matter changes. Teaching is a struggle to balance one's commitments while hoping to incite others to care as well. It is a form of activity in which caring about the context and conditions of the work, one's particular students, and the unpredictable promise of learning *might* all come together in satisfying ways. But often they won't.

It is not surprising, then, that many teachers settle on "doing their job" by fulfilling the basic duties asked of them as their principal object of care. Whether they fear the risks of caring, or are burnt out by having cared too much, or come to care about other things entirely, some teachers are reluctant or simply unable to sustain cares of more complex kinds. Still, many others welcome and embrace the stirrings they feel to care more deeply and, like Mor, press on despite the risks and disappointments that their particular objects of care bring into their life.

Why the Objects of Care Matter in Teaching

Who cares what teachers care about so long as they get the job done? Many people get by each day not really caring about the work that they do. Not all forms of work require caring employees to function well. I might detest accounting, but as long as I can crunch the numbers correctly and get my paperwork in on time, it doesn't much matter what I think about my job. In such cases, what I care about is not what the job involves. It is just the doing and keeping of the job that matters.

It should be clear by our account that we believe that teaching is not like this. There may indeed be teachers who, caring only about attaining the mandated achievement objectives required to keep their job, treat students as mere pawns in the process. But unlike accounting, whether a teacher cares or not about her students or about the subject matter directly impacts the quality of their work. Teaching does not allow for the kind of radical separation one finds in many kinds of work between care for the job and the stuff involved in doing that job, because in teaching the "stuff" talks back. Not only do students talk back, but the shape and direction of their lives, and the preservation of cultural practices, are partly affected by the cares of teachers. One's students, and usually not only them, take acute interest in what teachers care about, and to what degree. Even from the standpoint of a teacher who cares primarily about their job, the way that a teacher's care is expressed in practice, the kinds of things that motivate them and shape their sense of what is important in their work, resonates in everything that transpires. In all forms of teaching, the object and intensity of a teacher's care matters.

What teachers *ought* to care about is therefore a concern to many. A particularly exacting account of teaching is found in the work of the philosopher Hannah Arendt. She calls on teachers to love the world by preparing for its renewal and to love children by not leaving them to their own devices.[11] Expressing such deep commitments about the

---

[11] Hannah Arendt, *Between Past and Future* (New York: Penguin Books, 1993), 196.

world and about students has a powerful influence on both the lives of students and the preservation of worthwhile traditions and practices. While it may be true that many teachers find themselves closer to feeling ambivalence than love about what they do, there are obvious reasons why teachers should care deeply about what and who they teach. Arendt leaves us with two. The first is so that the traditions and cultural practices you cherish will continue to flourish. In fact, our oldest cultural traditions and practices would not have survived without committed teachers of some kind who conveyed such care, and in doing so passed down requisite knowledge, beliefs, habits, and skills to new generations. This is a compelling rationale for why we should care as teachers and about teaching in general. It is vital to our humanity and teaching naturally involves conveying one's cares and asking others to share in its meaning. But it is her second reason, caring about the well-being of one's students, that most concerns us here.

Care lies at the heart of social life. We are born into the language, customs, and hopes of our caregivers which, in turn, provide us with the form and content of our own life. Even as adults, our days are structured by care. We take care of our mind and body, we care about our appearance, immerse ourselves in our daily tasks, cultivate relationships with the people around us, and identify with the interests of what and whom we love. In fact, it is hard to conceive of anyone flourishing without being cared for and caring about something: the particular others, ideas, and things that matter most to them. Being cared for and developing cares do not happen only in schools, but relationships with and the work of teachers play a vital role in countless lives. Even without a sharing intent, students learn from their teachers and fellow students what is considered essential and inessential, worthy and unworthy of their time and efforts.

What role teachers *should* play is less clear. No matter how nurturing and supportive a school would hope to be, it is unavoidably limited and partial as to the cares of those who take part. Most teachers find themselves working in places that require at least some compromises with respect to their own cares—whether those cares center on the requirements and expectations of the job, the perceived needs and best interests of their particular students, commitments to the subject matter, or some elevated sense of what's most vital in the vocation of teaching itself. Teachers experience a tension in the necessary compromises they must make. But whatever their own cares and compromises might be, and how that works out for them in the course of their own lives, the nature of their work centers on what their students are expected to attend to and care about and the way in which the things *students* care about influences the course of *their* lives.

The impact of schooling on students is substantial. Hard choices have to be made about what matters and how much time and effort should be spent attending to one thing or another. While we often identify student cares through the lens of what teachers care about, it is vital that we also consider student cares and what might matter for their individual flourishing. Teaching, in fact, entails an ethics of attention: decisions must be made about what is worthy of attention and what can be ignored or dismissed. The ethical implications of what teachers care about are therefore profound and inescapable.

What, then, are we to make of the choices teachers make? An intriguing suggestion has been advanced by Robbie McClintock. Drawing upon ideas set forth by Plato at the dawn of philosophical thinking about education, McClintock conceives the issue to be about what he calls *formative justice*.[12] This notion differs from the way justice is usually understood in the literature on education. We are all familiar with distributive justice—addressing the concern that each citizen receives his or her fair share of material wealth and opportunity in an environment of finite resources. Political philosophers, lawmakers, social theorists, and activists of all stripes have concerned themselves with questions of distribution since the advent of modern society. Caring about distributive justice, as many teachers do, you will want

---

[12] Robbie McClintock, *Homeless in the House of Intellect: Formative Justice and Education as an Academic Study* (New York: Laboratory for Liberal Learning, 2005).

to ask what individuals are entitled to receive. In a school context, that might mean providing students with manageable class sizes, equitable funding, certified and experienced teachers, suitable conditions for learning, fair access to educational opportunities, and so on. These are critical facets of public education that make addressing distributive justice concerns vital to the survival of the institution.

Formative justice raises another fundamental question, best expressed in first person: How shall I develop my talents and potentialities in light of my limited time, energy, and resources? At its core, the idea is that what is most vital in education is a process of self-formation as each of us responds to the circumstances of our lives, in our own way, developing and drawing upon one's "particular mix of capacities and powers" to form a self and make one's way in life.[13] The work of teachers looms large in this process. Teachers have ideas about what is worth their students' care and attention. They also provide the environment in which many latent capabilities and interests are awakened, and they help shape the talents and powers a person has to work with as they go on in life. At the same time, what one actually cares about, and the clarity, confidence, and meaning of their caring over time, cannot be achieved without the active engagement of each student. Ultimately, every person must address this question and face the lifelong challenges of formative justice on their own. McClintock captures what is at stake:

> Guided, well or poorly, by formative justice, each person exerts educational effort to bring his or her mix of aptitudes to their full employment in pursuit of sustainable fulfillment. "Be all you can be"; this is the problem of formative justice that each youth must ultimately solve for herself. What do you want to become? What should you become? What can you become? How will you integrate the imperatives of desire, upbringing, and reason into a secure and fulfilling self? There is one life to live and a multiplicity of possibilities

---

[13] McClintock, *Homeless in the House of Intellect*, 77.

in it. Which merit realization, how, when, where, and why? This is the question of formative justice and good educational concepts, sound pedagogical principles, enable people to think about and act on such fateful choices. (78–79)[14]

Whether intentional or not, every teacher influences how these fateful questions of formative justice unfold, nudging students to realize some of their human potential, while leaving other latent capabilities underdeveloped or not developed at all. And we should in no way assume teachers impact the matter for the better. A curious and learning-delighted child can, under the guidance of certain kinds of teachers, become a narrow-minded, competitive overachiever, sitting alone on top of a world he no longer loves. Of course, it is equally true that a child, with a teacher's patient care, may find herself gravitating from fearful detachment to confident engagement in life, or from sullen resistance to noticing the delight of a poem, even beginning to write poems herself.

In this way, the elusive object of care that teachers strive to keep in focus matters greatly. Teachers must strive to understand and take action at the intersection of their particular setting, their students' unique characteristics, and the range of things it is possible to explore as subject matter. Those who choose to teach are willing themselves into the process in which their students are living their lives, and thereby adjusting the terms of formative justice, the journey of more or less fulfilling self-formation. As teachers we say to students, to really do justice to who you are and the potential you have—to make the most of your life (as I see it)—here is what you should work on and strive to do.

Most teachers care about getting this right, but recognize all the ways we can fall short or even lead astray the students in our care. Generating a sense of what is important also exposes one's vulnerability; there is unpredictability and risk associated with anything worth caring about. And the deeper one cares, the more susceptible one is to frustration

---

[14] McClintock, *Homeless in the House of Intellect*, 78–79.

and disappointment. One can care deeply and yet act in ways that bring harm to oneself or to those one cares about.

No one is immune to these risks, nor is there any getting around them. In their various and distinct ways, teachers model what it is to care. In doing so, teachers can and often do go wrong in all kinds of ways, or at least may seem to do so to those witnessing their work. Teachers, after all, are themselves engaged in the ongoing process of formative justice just as surely as their students are. In the circumstances in which they teach, they must reconcile what they care about with what they are expected to care about, then act in light of what seems to matter most. Some do justice to themselves and gain genuine satisfaction in that process of self-formation. Others struggle in a range of more or less tragic and instructive ways. But all teachers convey lessons of life in the process.

Problems of Care

Reflecting too closely on the impact of their commitments can lead conscientious teachers to self-doubt and other anxieties that their work surely warrants but rarely makes room for. By what right do teachers set about tinkering with, let alone transforming, the circumstances, capacities, and powers that shape the course of lives? What qualifies one to assume this responsibility? There are no easy answers to these questions. The standard response, that as teachers we are just doing our job in customary ways, won't get us very far. It is worth dwelling a bit more on the problems, and promise, of care.

In his famous commencement speech at Kenyon College, David Foster Wallace reminded recent graduates that what we care about defines us, and often in harmful ways:[15]

---

[15] David Foster Wallace, "2005 Kenyon Commencement Address." Accessed March 9, 2019. https://web.ics.purdue.edu/~drkelly/DFWKenyonAddress2005.pdf.

Worship power, you will end up feeling weak and afraid, and you will need ever more power over others to numb you to your own fear. Worship your intellect, being seen as smart, you will end up feeling stupid, a fraud, always on the verge of being found out. But the insidious thing about these forms of worship is not that they're evil or sinful, it's that they're unconscious. They are default settings. They're the kind of worship you just gradually slip into, day after day, getting more and more selective about what you see and how you measure value without ever being fully aware that that's what you're doing.[16]

The dangers of our commitments are plentiful, but he believes the objects of our care can also elevate and inspire. "The really important kind of freedom," Wallace continues, "involves attention and awareness and discipline, and being able to truly care about other people and to sacrifice for them over and over in myriad petty, unsexy ways every day."[17] Wallace locates the value of an education precisely in this freedom—an ability to think, to decide what matters in ways that lay bare and counteract the default settings of our everyday experience.

Teachers sometimes find such freedom in their work. And sometimes that work contributes to their students finding such freedom in their lives. In both cases, the freedom comes from acting wholeheartedly upon motives that one can fully embrace in oneself. For this to come about, certain problems and challenges must be faced. These arise from the fact that it is difficult in life to clearly realize and confidently affirm what one truly cares about. This may be especially true in the inherently complex and demanding contexts of teaching.

How teachers meet that challenge has real consequences for their students. Many teachers seem to care indiscriminately, either trying too hard to do it all or, perhaps having burnt out, seem to be adrift in the demands of the moment. Between these extremes there are teachers who find ways to clarify what they in fact care about in teaching. Doing

---

[16] Wallace, "2005 Kenyon Commencement Address."

[17] Wallace, "2005 Kenyon Commencement Address."

so informs their work with students; such teachers might be seen to stand for something, they are able to convey what is important to them. One can disagree with what they stand for or find important but still respect and learn from them. By being clear as to what they care about, students are afforded a glimpse of what such caring involves and what it means to act on the interests of something or someone outside oneself.

Regardless of the clarity of a teacher's convictions, setting out to impact the lives of others in ways that are the product of one's particular cares comes with great risk. For students and teachers alike, knowing when to care, what to care about, and to what degree are challenging matters in most contexts of teaching and especially in schooling today. Given the countervailing, external pressures on teachers with regard to what they are supposed to consider most important, combined with the vulnerability of truly caring about certain things outside their full control (not least of which are the students' own attitudes, desires, tendencies, and cares), the strains of the work are real.

Still, most teachers do not shy away from the entanglements of caring. They teach because they care; their caring supplies the more or less coherent reasons they need to carry on in practice. Their own fulfillment is bound up over time in the work of engaging students whose capacities and course of life they are determined to impact in some way. It is in caring about that that teachers return each day.

Why Care Matters

Without the sustaining motivation of certain objects of care, teaching would not exist; the activity, and all the elements comprising it, would be pointless. It is true that with so much teaching now institutionalized a non-caring person could play the part of a teacher, but for how long and to what end? Care infuses all the elements of teaching with some sense of importance, motivating the work of teachers. What those cares are, how deeply they are felt, and the ways they are acted upon in practice are all matters very open to question. Anyone can say what a teacher *should* care about, but it is what teachers *do* care about that matters, and what their caring conveys to those whose lives are most affected by their actions.

Thus, whatever its declared point and purpose, teaching is also an ongoing, sometimes confusing, and often contentious, display of caring in action. The capacity to care about things worth teaching, those one teaches, and the wider impact of one's work as a teacher all reflect a vital aspect of our nature as human beings. That such cares often become a jumble or misfire in unpredictable ways is no knock against care in teaching; it is simply the risk we all take in clarifying and acting upon genuine cares in what we do. For better or worse, one's teachers provide an object lesson in this crucial feature of life.

Thinking about your own experience teaching and being taught

- Considering the variety of teachers you have witnessed, how does what teachers care about (or seem not to care about) enter into and influence the nature of their teaching?
- How have teachers influenced what for you are important objects of care?

Thinking about conceptions and theories of care in teaching

- What is your view on caring? To what degree are Frankfurt's and Noddings' theories of care compelling?
- Does McClintock's concept of formative justice capture something vital that teachers do or should care about?

Thinking about care in other contexts of life

- Given current and emerging conditions of the world as you see it, what kinds of teacher cares are most important to express and act upon in teaching today?
- How important a role can or should teachers play in influencing what students care about in their lives?

2

Enacting Authority

"I have enough gunpowder in this jar to blow up this school," said Miss Lockhart in even tones.

She stood behind her bench in her white linen coat, with both hands on a glass jar three-quarters full of a dark grey powder. The extreme hush that fell was only what she expected, for she always opened the first science lesson with these words and with the gunpowder before her, and the first science lesson was no lesson at all, but a naming of the most impressive objects in the science room. Every eye was upon the jar. Miss Lockhart lifted it and placed it carefully in a cupboard which was filled with similar jars full of different-coloured crystals and powders.

"These are bunsen burners, this is a test-tube, this is a pipette, that's a burette, that is a retort, a crucible . . ."

Thus she established her mysterious priesthood.

Muriel Spark, *The Prime of Miss Jean Brodie*[1]

This vignette from the classic *The Prime of Miss Jean Brodie* is a rather dramatic example of what every teacher must do, to take some control of the situation and direct students' attention to the matters at hand. There is a variety of ways teachers strive (and sometimes fail) to do this every day. Some prefer to soften the power imbalance between teacher and students with good humor, abundant kindness, or an infectious curiosity while others rely on more direct means, a no-nonsense attitude, an intimidating presence, or simply the indomitable force of their sustained will and determination. That we can admire Miss Lockhart's theatrical virtuosity—her ability to utilize her surroundings

[1] Muriel Spark, *The Prime of Miss Jean Brodie* (New York: Harper Perennial, 1962), 80.

to maximum effect—without necessarily approving of her tactics or aims is testament to a simple fact that teachers know very well: without some degree of *authority*, teaching is all but impossible.

This fact is troubling to many. There's reason to bristle at the thought of teachers doing anything remotely like establishing a mysterious priesthood in a science class of twelve-year-olds. Perhaps you see it as a symptom of what is wrong with authority in teaching. We will take up such concerns, but it is nonetheless true that teachers cannot escape the need to establish some control and secure the respect and cooperation of students. No matter what terms we use to describe it, or how hard we try to democratize power relations in the classroom, authority remains an indispensable element of teaching.

This is not surprising. In fact, authority is a common facet of social life and in the development of persons. We are all born equally dependent on the experience and guidance of our first teachers— parents, guardians, and others nearby. At the outset of life this situation is defined by its fundamental asymmetry, children tune into those who not only embrace but also tower over them. At least for the fortunate ones, adults are there for them, carefully asserting their power over them in restrained, constructive, and nurturing ways. While children turn first to those who raise them, they increasingly rely on the guidance of other responsible adults, including teachers, to welcome them into the broader community, instructing them in its ways and practices. Learning to defer to the judgment of others is an unavoidable feature of social life. But such deference is desirable only up to a point. As we grow and mature, we all must learn to judge when and in what circumstances such deference is legitimate, and when it is not. Such judgments about authority are always open to question.

In this chapter, we want to suggest some ways to think about the pivotal role of authority in teaching. How do we experience and come to terms with this necessary but risky aspect of our lives? We begin our investigation with a detailed account of what authority amounts to and how it comes about. We are especially interested in the dynamic, relational underpinnings of authority in teaching, and in the fact that in educational settings, responding to teacher authority in the ways that we do, we develop to a considerable extent the ways of thinking about and responding to authority we carry into other circumstances in our lives. We then explore how, in taking charge, teachers assume responsibility for what transpires. Authority is an indispensable element of teaching, but as we shall see, it is also an intensely contentious one, an element both empowering and susceptible to abuse.

The Authority of Teachers

Think about examples of teacher authority in your experience. We probably can all recall teachers who possessed the kind of steady, unflappable presence of those who just seem to have it, the bearing of being in command. This doesn't imply barking orders; often authoritative teachers speak softly, conveying how secure they are in the role. What is the basis of such authority?

Standard thinking on the subject treats authority as a kind of possession, something one has and employs for certain purposes (indeed, our comment above about teachers who "have it" made use of this common understanding). This is true whether one has it on the basis of knowledge and expertise—those with some claim to being *an* authority in some domain—or on the basis of their position and office—those who are entitled to deference and perhaps obedience by virtue of being *in* authority. Examples are everywhere. Think of master mechanics, doctors, judges, or any category of people whose apparent possession of expertise, position, or both allows them to speak with or wield authority in certain circumstances. Teacher authority can likewise stem from either or both of these sources. But the notion that authority figures possess something by virtue of their position or expertise that grants them legitimate power over others doesn't clear up why and how authority works. After all, teachers with very similar levels of knowledge and institutional position can vary enormously with respect to the way they wield authority—with some falling short altogether. What accounts for the variability? To find satisfying answers to these questions, we should consider authority with respect to the way authority emerges in the dynamics of social life.

In a revealing analysis, Bruce Lincoln calls attention to the ways in which authority is a product of social relations.[2] In his view, it is best to see authority as the *effects* of distinct kinds of social context and interaction. The contexts of teaching and social relations between teachers and students would be prime examples. For him authority "is best understood in relational terms as the effect of a posited, perceived, or institutionally ascribed asymmetry between speaker and audience that permits certain speakers to command not just the attention but the confidence, respect, and trust of their audience, or—an important proviso—to make audiences act *as if* this were so."[3] What is Lincoln getting at here? Authority, he suggests, should not be thought of strictly in terms of the knowledge or institutional standing an authority figure possesses, but rather as *a range of socially generated effects*, certain patterns of response, whether genuine or feigned, that come about in the circumstances of certain kinds of interaction.

To illustrate, let's return to the opening vignette. The socially generated effects of Miss Lockhart's authority—that is, the degree to which her students believe and do what she wants them to believe and do—depend in part on her students' prior expectations of what a science teacher at this English senior school is entitled to do in this context.[4] In classrooms everywhere, teachers can expect some degree of student deference based on the "posited, perceived, or institutionally ascribed asymmetry" between the teacher and students that is reinforced over years of schooling. This contributes to the general expectation that students will not only listen to their teachers but also place some

---

[2]   Bruce Lincoln, *Authority* (Chicago, University of Chicago Press, 1994).

[3]   Lincoln, *Authority*, 4.

[4]   In the UK boarding school system, students attend senior school from age 11 or 13 to 18, combining what in the United States would be middle and high school.

confidence, respect, and trust in them (or, as Lincoln's important proviso suggests, at least act *as if* they do). Miss Lockhart's startling gunpowder comment relies upon that background of trust.[5] The truth is that simply being recognized as a teacher—however inept a teacher one might be—is enough in most classroom settings to endow one's words with a certain amount of authoritative force, an amount Miss Lockhart is determined to exploit for maximum effect. But even those students who are unimpressed with Miss Lockhart's opening strategy and have little interest in science or in her as a person will likely go through the motions of at least feigning respect, which is itself an effect of authority.

In addition to a teacher's institutional position, other factors of the context—from a person's race, gender, age, and social class to perceptions of relative ability and expertise—may impact how this asymmetry is understood and plays out. Miss Lockhart must have felt quite confident of her acknowledged standing in authority to utter the words she did: "I have enough gunpowder in this jar to blow up this school."[6] It is easy to imagine all kinds of circumstances in which such a comment would elicit a very different response. The point is that we all must learn to read the context in which authority relations unfold. The same basic features of authority play out when a road construction worker raises her hand to direct traffic, or when a doctor prescribes some treatment plan to follow. But unlike those examples, the context of interaction and potential range of responses that teaching involves is much more complex and often extends over long periods of time. The initial effects generated by Miss Lockhart's opening gambit set the stage for the further effects of the ongoing authority relations in her classroom to play out over time.

The importance of authority is that it provides for more or less stable, ongoing influence and control without having to resort to either force or persuasion, neither of which is practical in many domains of social life.

---

[5] This is a fictional account of a classroom in the 1930s. Most teachers can't get away with this today.

[6] Spark, *The Prime of Miss Jean Brodie*, 80.

Authority is nothing if not efficient. Across a wide range of social settings, including educational ones, protracted attempts at persuasion or acts of physical compulsion are often inefficient, counterproductive or just plain wrong. In fact, a strong reliance on either persuasion or coercive measures to motivate behavior is usually evidence of a breakdown in authority. When a teacher feels compelled to threaten punishments or spend excessive class time convincing her students of the value of the subject matter or the point of what they are doing, it is often precisely because she *lacks* authority in the eyes of her students and, unable to generate the effects of authority, must compensate in some way.

Given that authority reduces reliance upon both compulsion and persuasion—using force or providing reasons—how and under what conditions does it come about? Lincoln describes the optimal conditions in detail. It is worth reading the following passages with care, reflecting on what these conditions would be in all sorts of teaching contexts. Authority comes into play with

> the right speaker, the right speech and delivery, the right staging and props, the right time and place, and an audience whose historically and culturally conditioned expectations establish the parameters of what is judged "right" in all these instances.[7]

Consider how difficult it is to meet all these conditions and the variety of ways they might count as "right" or "wrong." For Lincoln, it is only when these conditions

> combine in such a way as to produce attitudes of trust, respect, docility, acceptance, even reverence, in the audience, or—viewing things from the opposite perspective—when the preexistent values, orientations, and expectations of an audience predispose it to respond to a given speech, speaker, and setting with these reverent and submissive attitudes, "authority" is the result.[8]

[7] Lincoln, *Authority*, 11.

[8] Lincoln, *Authority*, 11.

Viewed through Lincoln's lens, we can appreciate the artistry of Miss Lockhart's attempt to be judged "right" in these ways. We may of course have very different teachers in mind when we dwell on the skillful efforts of teachers we have known to get things right in these ways.[9]

Lincoln's account also suggests *the vital role students play in the effects of teacher authority*. Far from being passive recipients, the responses of students can range from reverence and genuine respect to varieties of compliance and feigned respect to aggrieved submission or more or less flagrant efforts to subvert and resist. In spite of a teacher's institutional standing and expertise, teacher authority is vulnerable to critical scrutiny, tests of will, and the shifting parameters of sanctioned behavior. Sometimes the most effective challenge to the teacher's authority arises not from open rebellion but from the students' decision to remain quiet and refuse to learn. This presents the teacher with the continual task of reading her audience and responding to the prompts and cues revealed in their behavior.

Lincoln's description also indicates that *each enactment of authority is unique*. This is not to say that authority occurs in a vacuum. Authority effects have a history and a teacher's and students' past experiences with each other impact how authority plays out in the present and future. But while the ongoing relationship between a teacher and students creates a pattern of expectations, and institutional settings generally depend upon and deepen such patterns, every new situation gives rise to a different confluence of factors, risks, and possibilities. Experienced teachers are sensitive to this fact. Miss Lockhart strongly suspects that her actions will silence her students as they stare at the jar in awe, but she can't be certain of this. Nor can she know the degree to which her presentation of impressive things will really sink in. And while it is true that teachers can often muddle through their lessons by leaning

---

[9] Sections of this analysis draw from an earlier paper, Paul Farber and Dini Metro-Roland, "The Promise and Limits of Online Learning: Reexamining Authority in the Classroom," in *Philosophy of Education 2011*, ed. Robert Kunzman (Urbana, IL: Philosophy of Education Society, 2012).

heavily on their institutional position or banking on past relationships of trust and respect, the effects of authority can subside or disappear at any time. To maintain the authority effects they desire, all teachers must continually respond to the specific demands of each new situation in ways that strengthen and renew bonds of trust and respect with their students, or at the very least, preserve the appearance of such bonds. The authority of teachers is therefore a deeply contextual affair. Striving to enact authority, teachers must concern themselves with that conjuncture of being "the right speaker" with the "right staging and props" in the setting, and responding to "the historically and culturally conditioned expectations" that lead their students to judge them as right in those ways.[10]

In this way, *the enactment of authority is also an inherently ethical matter.* What does it mean to get things "right" in these ways? And when is it right to affirm, question, even to subvert, the historically and culturally conditioned expectations that prop up established patterns of teacher authority? These questions direct attention to the power teachers have. It is a basic condition of education that students find themselves in asymmetrical relationships with those empowered to direct their learning and conduct. It therefore becomes an ethical responsibility of teachers to consider what lessons are being learned by their students about whom one should trust and respect, on what basis, and in what contexts. How should we think about this responsibility in teaching?

Questioning the Legitimacy of Authority in Teaching

We have provided a general account of how teacher authority works in practice. Authority effects are embedded in the work that teachers do, providing efficient ways for teachers to direct the learning and conduct

---

[10] Lincoln, *Authority*, 11.

of students. Students in turn develop attitudes and expectations about authority that not only impact them in the immediate circumstances but are also carried forward into other domains of life in which authority plays a part. In these ways, the power of teacher authority is clear and extensive. But what makes such power legitimate? That is an altogether separate question.

Given the varied and impactful effects of teacher authority, it is necessary to consider authority from both the teacher's and students' perspectives. What kinds of authority effects *should* teachers strive to bring about? What expectations of and attitudes toward authority figures and the power they wield *should* students possess? Or more to the point, what is a legitimate use of teacher authority? Without question, some domineering authority effects, and the habits of passive obedience or submissiveness they reinforce, would be judged illegitimate in almost any educational context. But it can be tricky to say what makes for appropriate teacher authority.

Think again of Miss Lockhart, her commanding presence regarding strict and high-minded conceptions of science and experimentation. She gained the trust needed to instill that vision in some of her students, but not in everyone. What a dry and pedantic academician she must have seemed to some, determined to extend the life of an elitist tradition or an exclusionary club. In every domain of teaching examples of this kind can be found. Think of the conflicting viewpoints about the effects of teacher authority with respect to the status of science, the nature and role of the arts, historical narratives of our disputed past, and clashing perspectives regarding our contentious present and visions of the future. And what about the social context of teaching? What are we to make of the centuries-long subjugation, assimilation, and exclusion of minority children by dominant cultures across the globe? Or think of the sexism and classism endemic to many cultures that would prescribe rigid gender roles to children or track them according to class expectations solidifying their place in the global economy.

Awareness of the scope of issues must if anything heighten skepticism about all forms of institutional authority. Drawing from the lessons of history, psychology, and human experience, it seems fair to assume that every enactment of authority entails the legitimation of some traditions at the expense of others. How we distinguish legitimate from illegitimate forms of authority is a matter of grave public concern. In a cultural climate that is generally wary of authority, a number of perspectives stand out in educational circles.

We see this clearly play out in extreme forms of student-centered pedagogy. Some believe that a truly liberating (and engaging) education can only occur when students are afforded the freedom to construct their own knowledge, value systems, and projects without the controlling influence of teachers or any official curriculum. Summerhill and its free school offshoots are early harbingers of this approach but it is not hard to find a variety of representatives in today's fiercely antiestablishment climate.[11] We find it in the unschooling movement[12] that champions homeschooling, in some constructivist[13] schools and classrooms, and especially in the libertarian[14] versions of cyber-schooling and online learning designed to severely limit, and in some cases completely circumvent, a teacher's influence on educational experience. To these critics, trust in the authority of teachers to shape educational experience harkens back to an earlier time when tradition—not freedom of

---

[11] Summerhill is a boarding school founded by A. S. Neil that reflects a radical student-centered approach. Class attendance is voluntary and students collectively determine and enforce the rules of the school. See Alexander S. Neill, *Summerhill School: A New View of Childhood* (New York: St. Martin's Press, 1992 [1962]).

[12] For an introduction to Unschooling, see John Holt, *How Children Learn: 50th Anniversary Edition* (New York: Hachette Book Group, 2017 [1967]).

[13] Constructivism: Philosophical perspective that treats knowledge as something constructed rather than passively received. There are a variety of forms of constructivism in education, starting with the pioneering work of Swiss psychologist Jean Piaget to more contemporary forms espoused by Ernst Von Glasserveld and Kenneth Gergen. For a useful introduction, see Leslie P. Steffe and Jerry Gale, eds., *Constructivism in Education* (New York: Routledge Press, 2009 [1995]).

[14] Libertarianism: As a political philosophy, libertarians believe in individual freedom and the limitation of government. In education, this usually translates as a challenge to state-funded schools in favor of the free market. For one such view, see Terry Moe and John Chubb, *Liberating Learning: Technology, Politics and the Future of American Education* (San Francisco: Jossey-Bass, 2009).

thought—dictated the beliefs and actions of the inhabitants of any culture. The paternalism and implicit collectivism grounding teacher authority deny students the essential freedom of movement necessary for self-actualization and a truly emancipatory education.

Not all critics go this far. Drawing from a strong tradition of liberalism,[15] many scholars seek to limit the heavy-handed exercise of teacher authority without denying its formative role in the development of persons. These scholars call on teachers to cultivate core liberal values, such as autonomy and critical thought, as a way to prevent indoctrination and mindless conformity in schools. They challenge the view that paternalistic forms of teacher authority can bring about an engaged citizenry rather than merely reinforce society's misdeeds, prejudices, and superstitions. Without a check on teacher authority and the persistent encouragement to exercise rational thought, they worry that we will raise a generation of citizens vulnerable to the extremes of anarchism and fanaticism. Or, as William Deresiewicz suggests, we will produce "excellent sheep," students who excel at taking tests and following formulas but show a diminished capacity for critically examining their own lives and the world around them.[16]

Here critical theorists[17] urgently weigh in. It is precisely because of long-standing patterns of inequality, stratification, and prejudice, and of the panoply of conflicting values and interests, that the authority of teachers is deeply problematic. When a teacher is the "right speaker," in the "right place," with the "right props," she can exert an unhealthy influence on her students and intentionally (or unintentionally)

---

[15] Liberalism: There are many forms of liberalism. In education, liberalism is generally associated with the cultivation of tolerance, autonomy, and independent thought. For one such approach, see Harry Brighouse, *On Education* (New York: Routledge, 2006).

[16] William Deresiewicz, *Excellent Sheep: The Miseducation of the American Elite and the Way to a Meaningful Life* (New York: Free Press, 2015).

[17] Critical Theory: This field of study has roots in German philosophy and the so-called Frankfurt School. Today, critical theory generally refers to an approach that seeks to understand and challenge various forms of injustice and oppression in society. For an introduction to critical theory, see Louis Tyson, *Critical Theory Today: A User-Friendly Guide* (New York: Routledge Press, 2015).

reinforce the oppressive structures of society. There are many ways things can go wrong. A teacher's expertise and understanding can be misinterpreted, overestimated, or abused. Even in the case of a teacher whose authority derives from widely acknowledged expertise, there is always the danger that students will simply accept what is being presented, and in that way, fail to do justice to the active role they ought to play in their own education. A teacher's authority can also keep students in their place—enter school as the son or daughter of working-class parents and leave as someone prepared for a working-class life. And what about marginalized students who do not feel, or perhaps even want to be, part of the dominant culture?

Critical theorists are impatient with claims that teachers in schooling today are or should strive to be politically neutral, and they ardently reject any kind of acquiescence in prevailing norms and traditions. In a profoundly unequal world, reproducing traditional power relations under the guise of political neutrality does not go nearly far enough to address our problems now. The point, as Karl Marx once remarked, is to change the world not merely interpret it.[18] From this view, the only legitimate teacher authority is exercised to emancipate students from inequality by encouraging them to actively fight against social injustice and oppression in all its forms. This is a future-looking, activist authority, not one caught up in the past or in preserving the status quo. Seen through a critical theory lens then, a teacher's responsibility is clear. Students should be encouraged to participate in change now, and in a way that is informed by the teacher's sensitivity to the most pressing problems facing society today. The focus of their attention might vary (e.g., race, gender, sexuality, poverty, immigration, the environment), but the dissatisfaction with the status quo and the call for action unite them all.

---

[18] The actual quote is, "Philosophers have hitherto only interpreted the world in various ways; the point is to change it." Karl Marx, "Theses on Feuerbach," in *The German Ideology* (New York: Prometheus Books, 1998), 571.

Assuming Responsibility

The critical perspectives we have introduced regarding the legitimacy of teacher authority do not repudiate the need for authority in teaching. After all, these perspectives are themselves kept alive by authoritative teachers. But broadly speaking, and for teachers across the wide range of institutionally supported teaching, these competing frameworks represent a deep challenge. Put simply, teaching cannot proceed without authority, but the conditions for assuming authority are inherently problematic and contestable. To find a legitimate basis for teacher authority in an age of widespread and often warranted skepticism, let's consider the role that teachers play in society today.

We all begin with the more or less attentive guidance of our first teachers. Many children spend the first several years of their lives in the small, intimate, and nurturing environment of a home watched over carefully by adults who count as family. We are not speaking here of some "ideal" domestic setting; there are all kinds of families and nurturing homes. For most children, there is no question of belonging nor of the bonds that bind family members together. It is here under the guidance of adult family members that children find their first footing. They learn to navigate their small private world with minimal intrusion from strangers. But there is also a larger, more diverse, and likely much less forgiving, public world out there. One way or another, children must enter this world and find a home in the wider community.

Historically, in growing up, the young have been subject to the authority effects common to those of their immediate community, caste, or station in life, as well as those ushering them into the guilds or practices associated with the outside world. But in the modern world, formal schooling has become a veritable rite of passage to adulthood for most persons. Teachers are now empowered with the responsibility of teaching unprecedented numbers of students across the globe. The way this responsibility is understood varies considerably, of course. But in every case, the modern institution of schooling bridges the gap between the insular private world of children and the expansive public world of adults. Teacher authority is legitimated, in part, by this pivotal role.

Perhaps the keenest observer of the legitimacy of teacher authority is Hannah Arendt. In her view, teacher authority is deeply grounded in a responsibility to deliver children into the common world, the result of which she calls a "second birth."[19] We are all born into a world not of our making, but it is only by learning about this world—our second birth—that we can take our rightful position among citizens and make *our own* mark on the world in unforeseeable ways. The teacher performs a vital role in this process. Arendt writes,

> The teacher's qualification consists in knowing the world and being able to instruct others about it, but his authority rests on his assumption of responsibility for that world. Vis-à-vis the child it is as though he were a representative of all adult inhabitants, pointing out the details and saying to the child: This is our world.[20]

In Arendt's view, teachers are something more than instructors of science, math, the arts, and so on. As representatives of the adult world, they have a duty to not only instruct students in their fields of study—the aspect of the world a teacher knows best—but also prepare them for an active public life.[21] This they can't do by means of wishful thinking or blind nostalgia; a teacher's task isn't to present the world *as it ought to be*, or how one thinks it *ought to have been*. Assuming responsibility for the world entails pointing out its many details to reveal the world *as it is*, warts and all, so that the young can one day make it their own. The justification of authority then is twofold. Teachers preserve the adult

---

[19] Hannah Arendt, "The Crisis in Education," in *Between Past and Future* (New York: Penguin Books, 1993).

[20] Arendt, *Between Past and Future*, 189.

[21] The term "public life" might seem like an oxymoron to readers of Arendt's work as she reserves the term "life" for the business of private living—caring for family, eating and drinking, cultivating private relationships—and "world" to refer to the shared traditions and public space of politics where citizens come together and act with and for the community at large. In this book, we will mark this distinction with the terms "private" and "public."

world by passing valued traditions down to the next generation while also preparing the young to renew the world as they become adults.

This might strike some readers as excessively paternalistic. And in at least one important respect it may well be—Arendt believes that if the norms, values, and traditions a community holds dear are to remain an integral part of society, then they must be protected from the blind ignorance, careless forgetting, and easy consumerism of the young. That is, the human world (in contrast to the natural world) doesn't preserve itself. Experienced members of society must assume responsibility for teaching the inexperienced about its values and practices.

But we shouldn't write off Arendt as a reactionary. Her vision is also radical in that by preparing the young for adulthood teachers pass on to them both the knowledge and the responsibility to engage with and ultimately transform the world in unique and unpredictable ways. In a democracy, this means that all students, and not just the children of the elite, must prepare for an active role in the renewal of public life. Without the first step of introducing them to the world, children are left to fend for themselves in a world that is largely alien to them, while the values and traditions that support public life remain defenseless against the whims of an ill-informed, throwaway culture. Without the second step of encouraging the next generation of adults to participate in the renewal of the public world, democracy degrades into a form of oligarchy whereby entire groups are excluded from participation and public life falters. Governed by hollow rules and lifeless traditions, public life becomes detached from the lives of most of its citizens.

Teacher authority is grounded in this dual commitment to preserve public life and our traditions and to prepare children for their active role in its renewal. Arendt concludes her analysis in dramatic fashion.

> Education is the point at which we decide whether we love the world enough to assume responsibility for it and by the same token save it from that ruin which, except through renewal, except for the coming of the new and young, would be inevitable. And education, too, is where we decide whether we love our children enough not to expel

them from our world and leave them to their own devices, nor to strike from their hands their chance of undertaking something new, something unforeseen by us, but to prepare them in advance for the task of renewing a common world.[22]

This is a heavy burden to carry for any teacher. It also raises some serious concerns about the parameters of authority in schools and its role in preserving democratic life and institutions. Even those inclined to agree with Arendt's educational vision have good reason to worry about how this might play out. It isn't even clear whether teachers should bear such a responsibility at all.

After all, this "common world" talk is highly contentious. Whose world is this? There is "our world" and multiple versions of "theirs," including the worlds of marginalized students and those incapable or uninterested in comprehending discussions such as these. How can we expect teachers to take that on? Moreover, while there is nothing in Arendt's vision that prevents teachers from representing the common world in all its diversity, engaging in critical thought and rational persuasion, or cultivating a sensitivity to issues of social justice, these anxieties nevertheless serve as reminders of the complexity and inherent risks of teacher authority. They also complicate our picture of what exactly *is* this common world that teachers are called upon to represent and preserve.

At the same time, if it is not teachers then who is responsible for preserving our cultural practices and traditions and for preparing students to take up their rightful position in the renewal of public life? It would seem that teachers play a vital role in this whether they realize it or not. As Arendt's vision makes plain, when teachers assume the responsibilities of teaching in the ways that they do, they enact authority and in so doing, they weigh in more or less responsibly on the public world.

---

[22] Arendt, *Between Past and Future*, 196.

Problems of Authority in Teaching

To those who find this talk of authority dismaying, it might help at this point to return to a few simple claims made in this chapter. Despite all the skepticism surrounding it, authority is an unavoidable feature of social life. Learning when, to what extent, and to whom we should more or less respectfully defer is an essential part of growing up. Even as adults, your prospects in life and the stability of your community depend in part on which politicians, journalists, doctors, friends, colleagues, and experts you place your trust in and on which ones you do not. There are times when challenging authority is the best recourse. At other times, it might be better to simply hold your tongue, feign respect, and for a time acquiesce. But for those who would benefit from relationships centered on warranted forms of expertise, learning how and whom to trust is required. At their best, such relationships can empower the young and inexperienced to do things they could not readily, or perhaps even ever, do on their own.

Authority is therefore not a problem to be solved, but rather is an element of life, and of teaching, to contend with, one that raises deep issues regarding its rightful use in various contexts. Without adults to take responsibility for the world as they know and care about it, there is little hope that the young will develop the capacity to renew the vital features of our world. On an individual level as well, one can hardly excel in any complex social activity or practice without suitable kinds of timely, authoritative guidance. But on both fronts, judgments about authority are inherently uncertain; we have all had to contend with the need to develop a capacity for discerning the indicators and parameters of legitimate authority.

From the perspective of the teacher at the level of practice, teachers can, and many do, approximate the most responsible possibilities of practice. They demonstrate what it means to be trustworthy. How does this come about? Consider the teachers you know and have known, or your own aspirations as a teacher. How do they, or you, face the range of issues, contending perspectives and unsettling doubts that would seem to overwhelm anyone who would wade into teaching today? There are of course ways to address the questions of legitimacy we have surveyed.

One way to respond is to simply hunker down. Tend to your own garden by focusing on your subject matter, the most secure basis of your authority, and leave the thornier aspects of education to parents and community leaders. There is something deeply appealing about this position. For one, it relieves teachers of the burden of being too many things to their students. It is not hard to come up with examples of teachers who overstep their authority and strive in one way or another to indoctrinate students to their own ideological persuasion. But complete neutrality in all things is impossible. Like it or not, all teachers, especially those of younger students, cannot avoid influencing their students in ways that extend beyond the curriculum. Teachers of advanced fields also find it difficult to separate their subject matter from the way in which their lives are led. Practically speaking, as we shall see in the next chapter, any position one takes, even a resolutely apolitical one, conveys messages to students about ethical behavior and to what kinds of things in the world it is worthwhile to give one's attention.

A second way that conscientious teachers address the issues surrounding their authority is to accept a somewhat more active role in the lives of their students. Teachers carefully nudge and redirect, leading students down paths that they think will be beneficial. Their authority may involve the expertise of assisting others to find their own way. Whatever the circumstances from which students come, and wherever they are headed, authoritative teachers often provide more or less useful guidance and instruction. Some teachers are a significant presence in the lives of their students in this way, role models representing the adult world in some ways, linking what their students do today to notions about the world in which they will take part.

Of course, this way of thinking doesn't reduce our anxieties about authority, it likely intensifies them. The worries expressed by libertarians, constructivists, liberals, critical theorists, and others are amplified whenever strongly held views about the full responsibilities and authority of teachers are advanced. Who after all has the "right" standing, in authority, to assume responsibility for what others are to learn or how best to orient them to the world that awaits? There is no good and settled answer to this question, though perhaps there are better and worse ones. It is an open question how the authority of teachers should be understood and enacted in practice.

Why Authority Matters

The questions we have taken up are not merely academic. Learning to navigate the parameters and effects of asymmetrical power relations is an essential part of being human. The quality of the "authority effects" we take part in and perpetuate, and the ways in which we learn to discern how and whom to trust in the diverse encounters with teachers, is of vital importance to our development as persons and our future orientation to all social circumstances infused with issues of authority and power.

Authority is thus both an ever-present and deeply problematic element of teaching. In assuming their role, teachers need to take some control of the situation and direct the students' attention to the matter at hand. The authority effects that result are both vital and unpredictable features of a teacher's work. For many teachers, evoking trust and genuine respect is a significant challenge. By virtue of the numerous settings in which we have been subject to teaching, we all have witnessed many ways in which teachers have assumed authority, and the many ways we have responded in turn. We can learn a great deal from such experience, even from those cases that in retrospect disturb us most. It is not uncommon that what we learn from these encounters is not exactly what our teachers intended. The larger question is what one learns about the sources of and ways of responding to authority in the many contexts of our lives.

Thinking about your own experience teaching and being taught

- Reflect on the range of authority effects you have experienced, from deep admiration to feigned respect or even some form of resistance. What accounts for the differences?
- How have such experiences impacted your life, for better or worse, and shaped your characteristic ways of responding to the authority of teachers?

Thinking about conceptions and theories of authority in teaching

- What are the most trustworthy indicators of legitimate authority in teaching?
- Do you find Arendt's justification of teacher authority compelling? Why or why not?

Thinking about how authority relates to the other elements of teaching?

- How does the strength of a teacher's cares impact her authority, and how does a teacher's authority influence in turn her ability to act upon her cares in practice?

Thinking about authority in other contexts of life

- How do your experiences of teacher authority compare to other kinds of authority you experience in your life?
- How might experiences of teacher authority influence (in both beneficial and harmful ways) how authority relations are understood and enacted in the wider contexts of social, political, and cultural life today?

3

Cultivating Virtue

Consider this scene.

> *Ms. Ryan's second graders are hard at work—being seven-year-olds dealing with schoolwork. Dependable Ana comes up to her and reports that Nate swore, three times he said "ass." Ms. Ryan knows that Nate can certainly be difficult, and she knows Ana is trying to be good. How to respond?*
>
> *Ms. Ryan asks Nate to come stand near her. He knows something was said about him; his face is reddening and his fists are clenched. Ms. Ryan tells him quietly that he is not in trouble, and asks Ana if she actually heard him say the word. No, says Ana, who indicates that Samantha told her. Samantha is asked the same question and says, well, no, but Anthony let her know. So Anthony, Ms. Ryan asks, what's the story? Anthony hesitates, then comes clean and says that he made it up. Ms. Ryan acknowledges his honesty and says she appreciates it. Nate returns to his seat, relieved to not be in trouble, this time—after all, he can be a pain in the ass—the girls recognize that they were played and played along. And the school day carried on. All of this, by the way, with 23 other kids in the background, a few watching the scene quietly unfold.*
>
> [Field notes from a classroom observation]

Moments like this are often brushed aside as brief distractions from the work of teaching, interruptions in the flow of meaningful activity. Nothing overly dramatic here, just an ordinary classroom moment with some heightened interest in which the intuitive expertise of a teacher displays a certain virtue in action. Most likely, her goal was to get things back on track, but in acting as she did, she also revealed the kinds of values that underlay her practical judgment and, in the process, may have also nudged a few children a little way down the path toward virtues such as kindness, truthfulness, and justice. Just another moment in a teacher's day.

Not all teachers would see and respond to the scenario above in the way Ms. Ryan did. A different teacher might have promptly sent the children back to work, with a stern glance toward Nate, perhaps, and a reminder to Ana to focus on her own efforts. Indeed there might be better and certainly there are worse ways one could have responded. No teacher is without reproach: each possesses flaws and their share of quirky ideas and questionable habits. In our diverse experiences, we look up to some teachers, tolerate others, and pity or even despise a few. But the point is this: teachers find themselves regularly confronting situations calling for some kind of "right response" where the right way to respond is uncertain. As a teacher you must act; even doing nothing counts as an action in situations like this. In responding to the social context, a teacher's virtues and vices are always on display. Teachers not only reveal something about their own character and the qualities that are bound up in who they are and what they do but they also seek to influence the character of their students.

This might make some readers uneasy. To teach anything beyond the official curriculum, let alone affect a student's character development, strikes some as a clear case of overstepping one's authority. But questions of value—of right deliberation and right action—are interwoven in the very fabric of social life. In just about every social context, we are all routinely called upon to make judgments about how to do the right thing or get things moving in the right direction. We also scrutinize the character of those around us. Being a good or bad friend, family member, or colleague is inescapably connected to the virtues one exhibits (or fails to exhibit) at significant moments in time. The need for diligence, honesty, courage, and self-control—the list of virtues can be readily expanded or amended—come into play in just about every aspect of life. Given the social nature of teaching and its inherent educative intent, teachers cannot avoid entanglement in questions of virtue.

To be sure, most teachers don't think of what they do as displaying or cultivating virtues. When teaching a lesson or addressing various situations in practice, teachers merely monitor what is taking place and, drawing upon their own character traits, act in ways that they believe will be for the best. Their striving to get things right in the situations of teaching models what for them is good judgment and right action, perhaps over time bringing out these qualities of mind and character in their students. Whether one is a master carpenter or kindergarten teacher, the cultivation of virtues is a constitutive element of teaching, even if it often escapes our notice.

In this chapter, we will take up three categories of virtue that are central to teaching: qualities that teachers routinely cultivate with respect to the integrity of a practice or discipline, the internalization of social norms, and the formation of ethical character. We then provide an account of how virtues of these kinds might emerge and develop in students under the influence of teachers. Our contention is that teachers play a vital role in the character development of students in ways that are often overlooked and underappreciated. Even under the most trying circumstances, the conditions for the formation of virtue in formal educational settings are present and such development, in fact, regularly takes place in the ordinary, day-to-day interactions between teachers and their students. We end the chapter by exploring problems of influence that come into view with respect to the ethical impact of teaching and some different responses such problems elicit from teachers and the public.

Sorting Out the Virtues

Some readers might have trouble getting past the term virtue, a term some associate with "well-ordered" classrooms, or settled notions of "good character" and a "proper education." A concern with virtue might also seem out of step with the current focus on scientific methods and measurable results. Why, you might wonder, bring up such an old-fashioned term at all? Perhaps it helps to state at the outset that this is not a moral guide. We are not offering here a particular list of essential virtues, nor do we argue that teachers are the paragons of virtue—or even that they should be. What we want to do here is convince you of the fact that teachers cannot avoid displaying something of their own character in their teaching or the need to develop certain desirable traits and habits in those they teach.

But first, what do we mean when we speak of virtue? Broadly speaking, *virtues are admirable traits of character,* distinctive kinds of excellence that are needed in response to the characteristic conditions and situations we face in life. Diligence is a virtue because life casts us at times into situations that require persistent efforts to overcome obstacles in the way of our success. While we do not all recognize or practice diligence in the same way, most of us have a general notion of what it is and value it in ourselves and in others. Julia Annas claims that to count as virtues, *such traits must be reliable, but not merely routine.*[1] Someone doesn't become diligent from one sudden burst of hard work, nor is being diligent mindlessly acting the same way over and over. Being diligent instead involves an emerging disposition to persevere in the face of a surmountable challenge, something which involves both a developing awareness of what kind of situations call for diligence and the readiness to respond, resist the temptation to give up, and demonstrate the right degree of resolve given the matter at hand. Such habits or capacities often develop and deepen over time with the guidance of a teacher.

What traits of mind and character do teachers regularly display and develop in their students? Let's examine three categories of virtue implicated in the practice of teaching.

- *Practical and disciplinary virtues* are traits of mind and character exhibited in the way one engages in activities related to some discipline or practice. Such virtues are the desirable habits of

---

[1]   Julie Annas, *Intelligent Virtue* (Oxford: Oxford University Press, 2011).

mind and action that help us excel in diverse practices or certain discipline-based fields of study, from accounting to zoology.

- *Mannered virtues* are character traits associated with the internalization of social norms. Formal learning cannot proceed smoothly without the observance of general social norms and dispositions that build a sense of community and promote a hospitable spirit of inquiry, conversation, and cooperation. Mannered virtues strengthen relational bonds and lay the foundation for the exercise of more specialized disciplinary virtues in teaching.

- *Ethical virtues* are those associated with the formation of ethical character. These virtues are the most controversial of the three categories of virtue in teaching. They are broader in scope and in an important sense they incorporate virtues of the other kinds, comprising those admirable traits and dispositions that speak to a person's overall character and the capacity to live a flourishing life.

Practical and Disciplinary Virtues in Teaching

Look closely at any form of practical activity or discipline-based field of study and you will find certain characteristics and traits that help make it what it is. Carpentry can't thrive without skillful carpenters who routinely exhibit virtues in ways that preserve and even advance the art of woodworking. The same can be said about other practices; there are recognizable and reliable ways to be a doctor, musician, and historian. To excel in each one involves knowing what the form of activity or domain of learning is about, what ends it serves, and how to bring others along in moving toward those ends. Depending on the practice or discipline in question, a number of broad human capacities become displayed in quite specific ways: diligence, self-control, attentiveness, truthfulness, respect for the efforts of others, perhaps even reverence for the tradition of activity in which one is taking part. Absent such practical virtues, the discipline or practice breaks down.

It is not surprising, therefore, that one of the primary tasks of teachers is to call attention to and appropriately display the traits of mind and action associated with their particular discipline or subject matter. Teaching any subject entails much more than simply passing down knowledge. Each one calls on us to apply virtues in distinct ways. Teachers both display and seek to bring out certain capacities needed to excel at a particular activity—responding to some text, solving for x, interpreting a piece of music. For example, conscientious teachers of history will model and cultivate virtues that reflect and sustain the practice of history as a way of knowing and understanding. They will exhibit a sensitivity to historical detail, an appreciation for and due diligence in seeking out a variety of perspectives and sources, good discernment in applying methods of historical interpretation and analysis, and a drive for truth that respects evidence, even when it conflicts with one's own point of view. A mathematics teacher might display some of these very same traits—attention, diligence, honesty—but do so in ways that better reflect mathematics' distinctive qualities and demands.

You might be wondering whether this can be said of all teachers. While such virtues clearly apply to the work of teachers who are deeply invested in some practice or domain of study, what about the many teachers who are not so inclined? They may teach mathematics or music, but do not identify themselves as, or display the practical virtues of, mathematicians or musicians. The gap is most evident in schools for younger children where a teacher's craft is sometimes only tenuously bound up with the subject areas introduced in the classroom. But perhaps even here there is concern with the cultivation of disciplinary virtues, especially if we consider the education of young children as its own domain of expertise. The development of a child occurs within a broad social context of emerging awareness of and engagement with valued cultural tools such as oral language and literacy, as well as various tastes, talents, and personalities.[2] Teachers carefully set the

---

[2]   Egan Kieran, *The Future of Education: Reimagining Our Schools from the Ground Up* (New Haven: Yale university Press, 2010).

pace and shape the environment in which a child will not only learn to read but also love the act of reading as well as care about new ideas and the people around her. Success is creating a small, safe place where students' latent capabilities can be awakened in stimulating and satisfying ways. Virtues such as curiosity, attentiveness, respect for the work of others, and so on are, and must be, well on the way to being developed before they can become fully evident in one or another field of study or practice.

For that reason, all teachers have responsibilities with respect to the cultivation of virtues relevant to the subject matter they teach—regardless of the depth of their own interests in it. We would rightly worry if young students were inattentive readers of literature or possessed neither the precision nor the patience to solve problems calling for basic analytic skills. Nevertheless, teachers exhibit respect for their disciplines in multiple ways and with various degrees of intensity. Most take seriously the challenge of helping students develop their capacities for ongoing, disciplined forms of activity and learning. The traits of mind and character displayed and developed in such efforts are a central preoccupation of their work, and a vital part of what teachers are expected to do.

Mannered Virtues and the Internalization of Social Norms

All teachers seek ways to establish and maintain the relational bonds needed for people to work together. They strive to create some sense of community. Without establishing norms of social cooperation, it is difficult to instruct students in any subject matter. This task is made easier by tradition. The norms of social cooperation are often already embedded in the culture of a particular group and social context. Consider how Ms. Ryan draws from a set of unspoken norms of honesty, respect, and patience to get to the bottom of the conflict. Teachers commonly lean on prevailing norms or established "good manners" when responding appropriately to specific situations and creating an environment for learning.

Of course, most teachers have at one time or another found themselves in the impossible situation of having to teach when these mannered virtues have broken down and a mood of irreverence, distrust, or even open hostility pervades the atmosphere. The effects are stifling. A teacher's authority is grounded in the acknowledgment of such social norms and the cooperation they can engender. It is for this reason that classroom management garners so much attention in schools and teacher education programs today. The need to establish at least some ground rules of respectful interaction, basic standards of decency, and a cultivated capacity for responsibility and cooperation is a critical part of any teaching experience.

These mannered virtues also form an integral part of the social and economic fabric of any community. Just as disciplinary virtues arise from the demands of engagement in particular disciplines, mannered virtues arise from the demands of the kind of society one is, or aspires to be, living in. John Dewey referred to such virtues as the "oil which prevents or reduces friction" but they play a more expansive role than that, especially in a flourishing democracy.[3] To reach decisions on thorny moral issues or address deep-seated antagonisms and conflicts requires a form of public engagement rooted in the norms of truth-telling, dialogue, and good will. The strength of communities also depends on virtues of industry and independence: we encourage students to work hard, be prepared, cooperate, compete, and persevere for the sake of the individual and the group.

Of course, the mannered virtues are also deeply problematic. While social norms can strengthen bonds of community and facilitate communication, they can also isolate outsiders, marginalizing those who cannot, or will not, conform to expectations. This is sometimes by design. The goal of a drill sergeant—a most severe kind of teaching, both in actual military settings and in teachers inclined to emulate the model—is to strip away individuality and dissent in order to create a cohesive group that thinks and acts as one unit. But this form of teaching

---

[3] John Dewey, *Experience and Education* (New York: Free Press, 1997 [1938]).

should be an exception rather than the rule, especially in a democracy. Without critical engagement and the possibility for cultural change, the mindless internalization of mannered virtues can destroy a community from within, reproducing existing inequalities and sowing distrust between subgroups. The overzealous enforcement of social norms can also prevent the kind of goodwill, creativity, and honest engagement that vibrant democratic communities require to adapt and thrive.

If done thoughtfully, however, the internalization of social norms need not lead to blind conformity. We introduce the young to the adult world, as Arendt noted, not in order to preserve the old unchanged, but to "prepare them in advance for the task of renewing a common world," a task that each generation must confront with the aid of whatever education their teachers and other willing adults provide. In fact, the mannered virtues can perform a double function here: they can reinforce social conformity and cooperation as well as illuminate contradictions in social life in need of correction. If civility and respect are worthy of emulation, then it becomes our duty to challenge aspects of our culture where incivility and disrespect reign. As Martin Luther King Jr., Mahatma Gandhi, Leymah Gbowee, and other courageous leaders have shown us, one of the most effective weapons of cultural change is to turn the expressed virtues of society back on itself. This can be done by revealing and actively challenging those instances when our actions are at odds with our declared principles, such as when students call out teachers for not living up to their own standards of responsibility, respect, and civility. What is essential here is that these and other activists are not calling for the eradication of social norms, but the refashioning of them to make society better.

Ethical Formation

"There are obviously two educations," remarked John Truslow Adams, "one should teach us how to make a living and the other how to live."[4]

---

[4] John Truslow Adams, "To 'Be' or to 'Do': A Note on American Education," *Forum* LXXXI, no. 6 (1886–1930): 321–27.

In addition to a teacher's evident concern to exhibit disciplinary and mannered virtues, teachers routinely call attention to *ethical virtues*— qualities and characteristics associated with notions of the good life broadly understood. Ethical considerations do not center on what is but on what ought to be. For teachers, it is the difference between focusing on those traits of mind and character that help us take part in the kinds of learning and sorts of community we happen to be engaged in, on the one hand, and those traits that are expressed in actions that advance what is good in itself. Ethical virtues derive from pondering how one should live, and find expression in actions that provide answers in the situations we confront.

In the opening vignette, Ms. Ryan may have acted out of a practical, disciplinary interest to get the students back to work as quickly as possible. She may have wanted to restore a suitable, respectful kind of classroom order. But then, she may have been moved by some deeper commitments—to truth-telling, kindness, and being fair—that she saw as being at stake here, and setting aside her curricular interests, responded in terms of the ethical demands of the moment.

Most observers would readily acknowledge the need for teachers to exhibit virtues of the first two kinds. But ethical virtues raise questions about the moral authority of teachers—the kinds of ethical stance they may be encouraging. The case of Ms. Ryan seems uncontroversial. But place a teacher with similarly strong ethical convictions in other situations. Can a history teacher, for example, distinguish the disciplinary virtues of historical evidence and argumentation from the ethical virtues of compassion or fairness when she addresses historical injustice and oppression? Should she strive to do so? In literature or science, where is the line between respecting prevailing norms of polite discourse and engaging in ethical judgment when confronted with the controversial topics of race or climate change?

Teachers have good reasons to be wary about overstepping the boundaries of their expertise. Engaging in ethical dialogue is fraught with risks and uncertainty. It can distract from the subject matter and disrupt the tenuous equilibrium so valued in educational settings.

Moreover, many teachers simply do not see it as their role to model ethical ways of life or encourage students to critically examine life. They prefer to concentrate on the subjects of which they are most conversant and leave the responsibility for ethical formation to the home or outside community.

Even those who encourage teachers to embrace this role and address ethical issues head on acknowledge its risks and dangers. In a speech to teachers, James Baldwin insists that

> the purpose of education, is to create in a person the ability to look at the world for himself, to make his own decisions, to say to himself this is black or this is white, to decide for himself whether there is a God in heaven or not. To ask questions of the universe, and then learn to live with those questions, is the way he achieves his own identity.[5]

Baldwin believes that teachers have a duty to educate their students this way, even though, he admits, doing so can lead to hostility and even resentment. When critically applied to the contradictions of society, virtues such as honesty, courage, and fairness can disrupt the social order. That may explain why we often wax poetic about the benefits of thinking for yourself and achieving your own identity at the same time that we make clear with our actions that "no society is really anxious to have that kind of person around."[6] Baldwin also warns teachers that students who routinely view society with eyes wide open may not like what they find. The worries do not end there. We probably all have known teachers who, while they laid a solid foundation of academic excellence, were ethically obtuse or indifferent. The danger of indoctrination is another concern. Teachers are rarely paradigms of virtue and the risk of wielding too much power over a student's life is real.

---

[5] James Baldwin, "A Talk to Teachers," in *Baldwin: Collected Essays* (New York: The Library of America, 1998), 678.

[6] Ibid.

At the same time, there is a reason why the ethical failings of plumbers do not trouble us as much as those of teachers. We rightly demand more from teachers—beyond the realm of their expertise—precisely because of the meaningful influence they *do* wield. Regardless of one's feelings about such influence, it would be a mistake to overlook the degree to which teachers impact the ethical formation of students. This is partly due to circumstance. As we saw in Chapter 1, schools naturally create conditions for ethical dialogue and identity formation. The daily interactions and relationships forged between teachers and students over long stretches of time provide rich soil for deliberation and action that calls for courage, charity, fairness, honesty, and so on. Moreover, teachers cannot help but model a way of life in attending to the things they care about. Thich Nhat Hanh, the revered Buddhist monk, put it this way: "Teaching is not done by talking alone. It is done by how you live your life. My life is my teaching. My life is my message."[7] While not every teacher aspires to do the same, they all display virtues and vices that students witness and, in many cases, emulate. Ethical issues inevitably emerge. How these ethical issues are addressed will influence students in a variety of ways, the effects of which extend beyond the classroom and the official curriculum into their public and private lives and relations with others.

The Unity of Virtue

At this point you might have noticed that our separation of the virtues into categories is somewhat dubious. In many cases, such as our opening vignette, the virtues interact in ways that make it impossible to say where one's attention to a discipline ends and ethical engagement begins. Indeed, this is precisely what needs to be recognized about virtue in teaching. Even the most clearly demarcated disciplines have infused within them all kinds of ethical issues that demand our fullest ethical attention and evoke

---

[7] Thich Nhat Hanh, *At Home in the World: Stories and Essential Teachings from a Monk's Life* (Berkeley: Parallax Press, 2016), 1.

the virtues involved (provided teachers in these disciplines are inclined to encourage such attention). Think, for example, of the profound moral issues that arise in and around various branches of science or technology today. Similarly, the social norms and mannered virtues of any group, especially the dominant one, raise ethical issues when they clash with the norms of other groups in a multicultural society.

It is no surprise then that recognizable virtues rarely fall neatly into one category or another. In fact, the hybrid nature of the virtues means, in part, that we can never completely escape the ethical domain. "The distinction," writes Jackson, "between being a good student and being a good person or between a poor student and a bad person is not easily drawn."[8] The same can be said of teachers. Whether our moral influence is consciously directed or not, students are highly sensitive to the character of their teachers; there may be little distinction made between a good teacher and a good person.[9] As some scholars of virtue suggest, while we can distinguish categories in order to clarify certain issues, there is good reason in the end to think of all virtues in terms of what they together bring to a person's life. Where teachers are concerned, this is probably good advice. Few teachers would feel satisfied with cultivating well-taught, well-mannered, and highly disciplined students who are well-positioned for a successful career if they were also callous or indifferent to the needs and interests of others.

In this section, we have made the case that the display and cultivation of virtue is an essential element of teaching. One simply cannot teach any subject well without modeling and developing core dispositions of excellence. In fact, the porous nature of the boundaries separating virtues makes it all the more important that teachers reflect on virtue of all kinds in their work.

---

[8] Phil Jackson, *What Is Education?* (Chicago: Chicago University Press, 2012), 86.

[9] Barbara S. Stengel and Alan R. Tom, *Moral Matters: Five Ways to Develop the Moral Life of Schools* (New York: Teachers College Press, 2006). Stengel and Tom discuss five different ways to develop moral life in schools. Our position most closely aligns with the integrated approach.

This leads us to a second contention. We believe that there is something about teaching, both in formal and in informal settings, that offers a natural way for the cultivation of virtues to take place. If this is correct, traditional schools and other formal educational settings of teaching can provide the conditions for the cultivation of individual and societal flourishing (or very different ends as the case may be). To see how this might work out in practice, we will need an account of how virtue is acquired.

The Cultivation of Virtue

It is not hard to see the virtues teachers display, but that is different from cultivating virtue in others, something that many teachers would downplay in their work or even deny altogether. So there is reason to be skeptical about our claim that teachers play a vital role in developing the kinds of virtues described in this chapter. You might even wonder whether character is something that can be taught. It falls on us to give an account of how this takes place.

Julia Annas offers us a compelling framework for thinking about virtue and its place in education.[10] She likens virtues to high-level skills that develop over time. One does not simply become virtuous. Rather, like the acquisition of some refined set of skills, such as playing the piano or learning to speak another language well, being virtuous is a gradual achievement that requires certain conditions to be met over an extended period of time.[11] Keep this skill analogy in mind as you read her description of how virtues develop over time:

---

[10] Annas, *Intelligent Virtue.*

[11] Portions of the section are taken from an earlier paper, Dini Metro-Roland and Paul Farber, "The Eclipse of Civic Virtue: Recalling the Place of Public Education," *Philosophy of Education 2012*, ed. Claudia Ruitenberg (Urbana: The Philosophy of Education Society, 2012).

Virtue is a matter of habituation but not of routine. To become kind or just requires learning how to deal with experience of various kinds for yourself and not just copying what someone else, or a book, says. You have to start off trusting your teachers to develop kindness and justice in you, showing you the right contexts and situations and teaching you in the right way to pick up what is important in these. But because your learning is not just mimicking but involves the drive to aspire, what you develop is a disposition based on understanding (to some degree, of course) of what it is to be kind and just, such that you can respond to new and even unfamiliar situations in ways that express what you have learnt from familiar ones. . . . Virtuous activity thus involves ongoing selective and differential engagement with the world, not a repetition of a routine once learned and then safely relied on.[12]

A few observations are worth noting. The first involves the importance of a *teacher-student relationship*. By teacher, Annas is here referring to *anyone* who is recognized as having character traits worthy of admiration. Of course, teachers do not necessarily possess such traits simply by virtue of being teachers, but they are routinely put into situations where they must display their character and respond to events in ways that might capture students' attention, and suggest admirable forms of conduct. Ms. Ryan's concerted interest in kindness, honesty, and justice may well have had an effect on those present. Wittingly or not, the nature of teaching creates the conditions for teachers to serve as role models of good conduct.

Another observation is that the learner must have *adequate opportunities to practice virtuous activity*. It is only after years of responding to different situations that students can progress from merely copying the behavior of their teachers to responding to situations appropriately on their own. Ms. Ryan's interaction with her students is, at best, only the beginning, one instance of a chain of events where such virtues would come into play, gain notice, be

---

[12] Annas, *Intelligent Virtue*, 74.

deliberated on, and applied. As her students go on to grapple with the implications of such notions in their own conduct, their horizons of possibility widen and develop. Ideally, this process would lead students not only to independence—no longer needing to rely on role models for guidance—but possibly also to their becoming role models for others to emulate in turn.

The development and practice of virtue demands both the intellect and the *aspiration of the learner*. Like authority, the cultivation of virtue doesn't occur without consent. Yes, students are molded by their environment—the source of their life options and aspirations—but the habits they acquire and the person they become are partly dependent on where their aspirations and attention lead them. For one to be virtuous, one doesn't just do what is right or what one is told, one must do the right thing for the right reasons and with the right desire. Learning how to do this requires more than mindless rule-following; it requires both heightened attentiveness and active commitment.

Initially, this engagement takes on a superficial, forced quality. None of the children in the opening vignette was disposed to get at the truth or treat Nate justly, except the teacher. In responding as she did, a nudge was given to the idea of acting on impulses of a different kind, the aspiration to figure out and do the right thing. The force of the nudge in this case was the fact that the teacher's actions toward Nate had weight for those involved; they cared what she was thinking and how she responded. Eventually, the feelings and aspirations of students will tend to align with the kinds of virtue they witness, traits that they become disposed to develop in themselves and to act upon when circumstances call for them to act virtuously in those ways. Various traits become internalized over time, which is why it matters how teachers think about and act upon the virtues they display.

Like learning a high-level skill, this process of internalization often escapes our notice. Mark Edmundson's recollections of playing high school football capture this initial, awkward phase, where the real significance of what is learned often does not occur to students until much later. Despite what he believed at the time, the objective on the deepest level, he later realized, "wasn't to score touchdowns or make tackles or to block kicks," but to perfect the art of practice.

> And practice was about trying to do something over and over again and failing and failing and failing and then finally succeeding partway. Practice was about showing up and doing the same drills day after day and getting stronger and faster by tiny, tiny increments and then discovering that by the end of the season you were effectively another person.[13]

A similar process occurs as one learns a new language. The beginner awkwardly stumbles through conversation, straining to recall the proper word and speak with the correct grammar and pronunciation, while the fluent speaker uses the language as an extension of herself, adroitly expressing her feelings and delivering the appropriate responses to her conversation partner's queries. What seems like a cold and foreign world to the beginner becomes a comfortable home to the advanced speaker as she learns to think, feel, and dream in her newly adopted language.

In the development of virtue, as in the honing of high-level skills, the move from beginner to expert does not happen overnight. Over time, one needs opportunities to witness and employ situated reasoning, encouragement with respect to aspirations to virtue, and the experience of authentic relationships that help one become accustomed to a variety of complex social patterns and situations that test one's traits of mind and character. Teachers play a pivotal role by way of the examples they set as their own qualities are put on display every day. In fact, the many years of schooling provide natural conditions for sustained teacher-learning relationships and the development of diverse qualities of mind and character. That after a year of practicing football Edmundson became another person—and not just an upgraded football player—suggests the power of formal and informal teaching practices to shape

---

[13] Mark Edmundson, *Why Football Matters: My Education in the Game* (New York: Penguin, 2014), 35.

the character of those involved. Of course, teachers are capable of displaying and influencing the habits and dispositions of the young in both good and bad ways, whether intentionally or not. Teaching, as we have argued these first three chapters, is never ethically neutral.

Problems of Virtue

Plato famously claimed that "the bent given by education will determine all that follows."[14] He might have exaggerated the extent of its influence, but it is hard to argue with his point that education—and by extension schooling—has a profound moral and intellectual impact on children. It is therefore vital that teachers understand the degree to which they can affect so many domains of life, from disciplinary excellence, civic engagement and social acceptance, to the variety of ways one can live the good life. As Jackson noted, "it's there that so many lifelong attitudes and dispositions take root and flourish or, conversely, wither on the vine."[15]

It is therefore not surprising that teachers worry about the influence they have on their students, and whether they are up to the task or sensitive enough to the potential ramifications of shaping, or even transforming, the character of their students. Certain historical facts justify this unease. In most culturally diverse societies, schools have a long and troubled history of indoctrinating students to serve questionable state and local interests. A respect for pluralism will therefore lead many teachers to actively avoid entanglement in ethical concerns. Many teachers do not feel capable of or inclined to represent anything beyond their field of expertise. There are too many ways it has gone and can go wrong.

The teacher's perspective is hardly the only one that matters in deciding what virtues should be modeled and developed in schools.

---

[14] Plato, *The Republic of Plato*, trans. James Adam (Cambridge: Cambridge University Press, 1902), 425:b.

[15] Philip Jackson, *What Is Education?* 86.

There is a range of perspectives that bear on this issue in direct and indirect ways. In no particular order, teachers must acknowledge the role of the state, the vast, multilevel regulatory and governing system of institutional demands and expectations regarding their work. Then there is the global network of economic and market forces, which increasingly frames the activity of schools and all kinds of teaching. Much closer, there are the parents and loved ones of those being taught, with their many and various hopes and concerns. And, of course, there are powerful forms of religious and cultural influences, belief systems, and ways of life that contend for prominence in debates about the kinds of virtues teachers should model and cultivate.

Complicating things further is the paradoxical nature of education itself. James Baldwin locates this paradox in two conflicting visions of education. An education that entails cultivating the "ability to look at the world for himself" and render ethical judgments runs counter to the task of socializing students to uncritically accept the norms, ideals, and self-image of society.[16] The former almost always gives way to the latter in institutional settings. Critical thought and independence may be prized in theory, but one is rarely encouraged to practice them in schools. This is especially true, remarks Baldwin, for marginalized students whose awareness of their marginalization—in terms of race, ethnicity, gender, and sexual orientation, for example—and questioning of the founding myths of the dominant culture reveal gaps and failures in society's universal aspirations of tolerance, decency, and fairness.

Given the problematic nature of virtue, it is understandable why many downplay the significance of virtue in teaching. Administrators and policymakers taking a managerial approach to school learning seek to do this in one of two ways.[17] The first strategy, best exemplified

---

[16] Baldwin, *Collected Essays*, 678.

[17] Managerial Approach to Education: The view that schools should be run using scientific principles of organization and accountability to consistently meet measurable learning outcomes. A particularly influential version of this view is found in Ralph Tyler, *Basic Principles of Curriculum and Instruction* (Chicago: University of Chicago Press, 2013 [1949]).

by proponents of online instruction, calls for a shift to more efficient delivery systems that decenter a teacher's authority, minimize non-curricular interactions and relationships, and focus attention on targeted skills, standards, and bodies of knowledge. As the teacher and the complex moral life of the classroom become expendable, education is reduced to information transfer and the developing of discrete skills.

The second strategy is evident in most brick-and-mortar schools where moral education is formalized in the service of institutional imperatives. Here moral education is often reduced to a form of behavior modification that lends itself more to the efficient working of the system than to any thoughtful treatment of the ethical development of its students.[18] Controversy is avoided at all costs, and authority depends more on institutional position and one's adherence to program fidelity rather than the trust and respect earned in the classroom from direct involvement in ethical issues as they arise. In both responses, concerted efforts are made to prevent teachers from wielding ethical influence over their students. The first severely restricts (and in some extreme cases eradicates entirely) the role of teachers, while the second neutralizes the impact of the value commitments and virtues of teachers and minimizes risk through impersonal scripts and protocols.

Neither response is likely to succeed in eliminating the formative role that teachers play in the moral lives of their students. For one, it is difficult to acquire expertise in a field without also acquiring the array of disciplinary and mannered virtues displayed and cultivated by teachers. Online instruction can only take one so far.[19] System-wide character education programs also fail unless teachers can build relational bonds and meet objectives creatively and organically. There

---

[18] Some of the ways this happens is presented in Stengel and Tom, *Moral Matters*.

[19] We see evidence of this in the low completion rates of online schools in the United States, where "the graduation rates of 50.7% in virtual schools and 49.5% in blended schools fell far short of the national average of 83%." Gary Miron, Christopher Shank and Caryn Davidson, "Report Full-time Virtual and Blended Schools: Enrollment, Student Characteristics, and Performance," *National Education Policy Center* (Coulder, CO: National Education Policy Center, May 2018).

is reason to believe that many teachers will routinely go off script and engage in ethical dialogue and action when the situation calls for it. Most teachers are invested in truth-telling, they believe in the intrinsic worth of their practice or discipline, and care that students critically engage with the content in ways that have a direct impact on their lives.

Most likely a balance needs to be sought. After all, some form of order and control is necessary in order for teaching and learning to take place. Where authority breaks down, you are likely to have chaos rather than meaningful freedom. But it is hard to deny the vital importance of ethical engagement in education—even if it occasionally disrupts the planned order of things. No matter how many short-term benefits social and curricular conformity bring, without honesty, critical dialogue, and healthy forms of innovation societies and cultures perish. Where virtue is concerned, education both preserves the status quo and provides the conditions for its renewal and change; this is a tension in all teaching where virtue is concerned.

There are all types of teachers of course and many ways in which they navigate these turbulent waters. How well they do is an open question; a teacher's courage, in delving into an emotionally sensitive, controversial issue, may be praised by some and harshly criticized by others. Indeed, the teacher may question it herself after the fact. That is the nature of virtue. Even in the most trying circumstances, it is possible for teachers committed to some form of goodness to create authentic relationships and embody models of excellence just as the hypocrisy of others acting in similar circumstances highlights human shortcomings, sometimes in an unintentionally instructive way.

Why Virtue Matters

We return once again to our opening vignette and our contention that the cultivation of virtues is not something that can be undertaken quickly nor achieved through canned lessons and behavioral formulas alone.

The most common normative influences on students are not primarily found in character education programs or classes on ethics or civics. They emerge in relational bonds and daily interactions between teachers and students, where virtues are modeled, practiced, and internalized over an extended span of time. Ms. Ryan's subtle moral instruction would have no effect without prior and subsequent modeling, practicing and internalizing, and without the moral authority she had established with her students in practice. It is impossible to deny the risk of such influence and there is no way to predict what a teacher's impact will be. The cultivation of virtue is a fact of life for cultural beings, an unavoidable and deeply contested region in the landscape of teaching.

The place of virtue in teaching is as uncertain and ambiguous as it is in modern culture overall. We all want virtuous leaders, professionals, businesspeople, and indeed virtuous friends, family members, and neighbors. But what good character looks like in the many, overlapping contexts of modern life is open to interpretation. The language of virtue resonates, but what the words mean is debatable. Still, in teaching, one doesn't merely use the language, one acts upon and displays certain traits of mind and character that play a part in the way those being taught understand and come to act upon virtue in their lives.

Thinking about your own experience teaching and being taught

- What in your experience are some of the most prominent or important virtues teachers regularly display and cultivate?
- How have these traits and qualities, or their absence in some cases, affected your own sense of virtue and good character?

Thinking about conceptions and theories of virtue in teaching

- To what degree are the disciplinary, mannered, and ethical virtues interconnected?
- In what way is Annas' account of the development of virtues as a kind of achievement or development of skills true to your experience?

Thinking about how virtue relates to the other elements of teaching

- What relationship do you see between what teachers care about and the virtues they display and cultivate?
- How is teacher authority tied in some way to the virtues on display in a teacher's work?

Thinking about virtue in other contexts of life

- What role, if any, do you believe teachers should play in the formation of their students' character outside the classroom?
- What issues, problems, and possibilities do you see with regard to the broader social impact of cultivating mannered and ethical virtues in schools?

4

Interpreting Subject Matter

That time of year thou mayst in me behold
When yellow leaves, or none, or few, do hang
Upon those boughs which shake against the cold,
Bare ruined choirs, where late the sweet birds sang.
In me thou see'st the twilight of such day
As after sunset fadeth in the west;
Which by and by black night doth take away,
Death's second self, that seals up all in rest.
In me thou see'st the glowing of such fire,
That on the ashes of his youth doth lie,
As the deathbed whereon it must expire,
Consumed with that which it was nourished by.
This thou perceiv'st, which makes thy love more strong,
To love that well which thou must leave ere long.

William Shakespeare[1]

"Mr. Stoner, what does the sonnet mean?"
    Stoner swallowed and tried to open his mouth.

"It is a sonnet, Mr. Stoner," Sloane said dryly, "a poetical composition of fourteen lines, with a certain pattern I am sure you have memorized. It is written in the English language, which I believe you have been speaking for some years. Its author is William Shakespeare, a poet who is dead, but who nevertheless occupies a position of some importance in the minds of a few." He looked at Stoner for a moment more, and then his eyes went

---

[1] William Shakespeare, "That time of year thou mayst in me behold" (Sonnet 73), in *Arden Shakespeare Complete Works* (London: Thomson Learning, 2001), 30.

blank as they fixed unseeingly beyond the class. Without looking at his book he spoke the poem again; and his voice deepened and softened, as if the words and sounds and rhythms had for a moment become himself:

> *"That time of year thou mayst in me behold ...*
> *To love that well which thou must leave ere long."*

In a moment of silence, someone cleared his throat. Sloane repeated the lines, his voice becoming flat, his own again.

> *"This thou perceiv'st, which makes thy love more strong,*
> *To love that well which thou must leave ere long."*

Sloane's eyes came back to William Stoner, and he said dryly, "Mr. Shakespeare speaks to you across three hundred years, Mr. Stoner; do you hear him?"

William Stoner realized that for several moments he had been holding his breath. He expelled it gently, minutely aware of his clothing moving upon his body as his breath went out of his lungs. He looked away from Sloane about the room. Light slanted from the windows and settled upon the faces of his fellow students, so that the illumination seems to come from within them and go out against a dimness; a student blinked, and a thin shadow fell upon a cheek whose down had caught the sunlight. Stoner became aware that his fingers were unclenching their hard grip on his desk-top. He turned his hands about under his gaze, marveling at their brownness, at the intricate way the nails fit into his blunt finger-ends; he thought he could feel the blood flowing invisibly through the tiny veins and arteries, throbbing delicately and precariously from his fingertips through his body.

> *Sloane was speaking again. "What does he say to you, Mr. Stoner? What does the sonnet mean?"*

John Williams, *Stoner*[2]

---

[2]   John Williams, *Stoner* (New York: New York Review Book, 2003 [1965]), 12–13.

The vignette offers a classic scene of college teaching circa 1940: An old literature professor with the stodginess of his generation poses a question and a skinny, introverted farm boy characteristically fumbles for the right response. The subject matter, a Shakespearean sonnet, serves to unite these two unlikely partners in a dialogue of sorts. But about what exactly? Is the poem merely an elaborate prop to illustrate "a poetical composition of fourteen lines," or a nod to the most famous writer of the English language, or is there some hidden, deeper meaning lodged in the sonnet itself?

The authority of the teacher is clearly established. Sloane's commanding grasp of the sonnet and professorial demeanor secure his position as the representative of tradition in the room. It is assumed by all that his familiarity with the subject matter is extensive. Sloane's voice, deep and soft, indicates a reverence for the poem. Whatever is going on here, it seems that it all comes down to the question that Sloane poses: *What does he say to you, Mr. Stoner?* For Stoner, this moment will be transformative.[3]

Others might have taken away something else from this encounter: from notions about Shakespeare's place in the canon of English literature to contempt for such canons. Be that as it may, his teacher, Professor Sloane, does what all teachers must do, he strives to *impart some subject matter to students.* This element of teaching is in many ways the most obvious; subject matter lies at the heart of teaching. To many, it represents a clear and solid object of attention in an otherwise opaque and fluid practice. After all, it's the subject matter and the students' grasp of it that matters most. But upon closer inspection, we will find that the subject matter is not as clear-cut as it may at first seem.

It is our contention in this chapter that the common goal of teachers—to impart the subject matter to students—is not a mere transfer of information or replication of skill. Seeing it that way conceals the inherent dynamism and unpredictability of both the

---

[3] Williams, *Stoner*, 13.

nature of the subject matter itself and the process by which it is conveyed and understood. Instead, teachers and students are faced with a *fundamentally interpretive task* of making sense of the subject matter. To illuminate what this task is, we provide a theory of understanding. The context for this is the sheer complexity of the many kinds of knowledge and know-how that constitute the subject matter. We then end with a commentary on the problems of the subject matter as they relate to this interpretative process and the many ways it matters, not just to teachers but in one way or another to their students as well.

On Making Sense of Subject Matter

"The primary difference between our species and all others," argues Daniel Dennett, "is our reliance on cultural transmission of information and hence on cultural evolution."[4] Throughout the history of humankind, teaching, alongside imitation, has proven to be the most effective means of passing down our cultural inheritance to new generations. No other species on earth participates in a form of teaching that can disseminate complex subject matter drawing from various cultural traditions and practices across such vast distances in time and space.[5]

One can imagine that in prehistoric times what primarily counted for our cultural inheritance, the subject matter worthy of being taught, was directly related to group sustenance and survival—in making and using tools, finding and preparing foods, building and maintaining shelter. The spiritual role that art and religion played in these early communities must remain something of a mystery. Yet since recorded history, civilizations throughout the world have been nourished

---

[4] Daniel Dennett, *Darwin's Dangerous Idea* (New York: Touchstone, 1995), 331.

[5] Thomas Suddendorf, *The Gap: The Science of What Separates Us from Other Animals* (New York: Basic Books, 2013), 165.

by various traditions and practices that extend well beyond the imperatives of survival. Religion, art, history, and literature emerged alongside politics and technologies of agriculture and industry to not only transform the physical environment but also establish richly textured cultural worlds. With the advent of the printing press and the rise of mass literacy, the impact of many of these cultural traditions and practices spread across distant lands with astonishing speed and efficiency. People were increasingly exposed to a greater diversity of knowledge, skills, and beliefs from many sources outside their small, face-to-face communities.

Today, what can count as culture, and the various traditions and practices that give it its shape, is so vast and incomprehensible that to speak of a common curriculum or what everyone should know in order to be recognized as an educated member of society strikes many as naïve if not completely misguided. There is simply too much content to choose from and no good way to determine which aspects of our traditions and practices are worthy of being passed down and which ones should be disregarded or challenged. Furthermore, libraries everywhere and all kinds of cultural content are increasingly part of the digitized, searchable world, widely available to interested learners. Subject matter, it seems, is everywhere. But from everything that is in principle accessible, how much is actually noticed and brought to life in some way? How do we determine what is worth our care and attention?

This is where teaching comes in. Among the elements of teaching, subject matter is in some sense the most obvious one; teaching is always teaching about something, the content is always present, whether it is some substantive material captured in books, libraries and the internet, or certain fundamental cultural tools, such as language, literacy, numeracy skills, and other sophisticated methods of inquiry and communication. The question is what in particular should teachers focus upon in their teaching and why.

Here the teacher's role of mediator comes into view. Broadly speaking, teachers place themselves (or are placed) in the middle between the vastness of cultural traditions and practices, on the one hand, and their students with respect to everything they might develop the capacity to know, do, appreciate, renew, and understand, on the other. Teaching thus requires two curricular tasks. One involves determining what the subject matter is or ought to be, out of everything in the world it might contain. The other involves making sense of the subject matter for oneself while also paying attention to how it will likely be understood by and impact one's students. Let's briefly take up these two tasks in turn.

What to Make of Subject Matter

The first task teachers face concerns selecting the subject matter. At first blush, this may seem simple. School subjects and the kinds of knowledge and skills basic within them are very familiar features of schooling around the world. In fact, for countless teachers, this task is already done for them. Today textbooks and established curriculum guides map out what is to be taught without the teacher's input. The selection of the subject matter becomes a foregone conclusion. But is it as simple as that?

In "Two Dogmas of Curriculum," Jane Roland Martin challenges two general misconceptions regarding the curriculum.[6] The first, what she calls the Dogma of God-given Subjects, refers to our tendency to treat the subjects of the curriculum as "givens" that are found and not made. We come to also assume that "the 3Rs [reading, writing, and arithmetic], the sciences, foreign languages, the humanities, the fine arts—are the only subjects there are."[7] In doing so, we often fall prey to a second misconception, the Dogma of the Immutable Basics, by treating the basic skills of reading, writing and arithmetic as unchanging, eternal, and *the* necessary conditions for learning anything else of value. Martin believes that both dogmas distort our conception of the curriculum

---

[6] Jane Roland Martin, "Two Dogmas of Curriculum," *Synthese* 51, no. 1 (Apr., 1982): 5–20.

[7] Martin, "Two Dogmas," 5–6.

and prevent us from properly understanding our relationship to subject matter.

Subjects, Martin insists, are *human constructions*; they are made through a creative process that continually evolves. Subject matter is therefore *endlessly open to interpretation*. There is a lot at stake in determining what it is we value and how we understand the relationship between the subject matter and the outside world. "The decision of what to make the basics of education, like every major curriculum decision, depends not simply on the way the world is but on the way we think it should be, on the kind of life we believe to be worth living, and on the kind of society we believe to be worth living in."[8] Martin isn't here suggesting that we do away with subjects altogether or stop teaching the "3Rs." What she is calling on us to do is to acknowledge that determining what the subject matter is and how it is to be understood are more complex and unsettled than is generally portrayed; the traditions that we draw from in creating the subject matter shift and evolve in the context of social-historical and cultural developments of all kinds. It falls on us to interpret what is of value in the ever-changing landscape of cultural ideas, products, and developments so that we might design our curricula accordingly.

The "us" in that last sentence is important. Teachers aren't the only ones who weigh in on this issue. For millions of teachers in schooling today, the subject matter is guided and constrained by an institutional context of school administration, often itself accountable to a wider framework of governmental mandates and regulations and the industry that markets curriculum materials based on prevailing standards. The particular history and scope of such managerial, political, and economic influences will vary from country to country and often domestically within states and regions. Part of a teacher's mediating role involves the recognition and interpretation of such mandates and administrative guidelines regarding subject matter, as these filter

---

[8] Martin, "Two Dogmas," 18–19.

down through formal channels as well as the more informal influence of conventional approaches and ideas about what they teach. Making sense of the vast industry of instructional materials, texts, workbooks, and other packaged subject matter content adds further complexity to the teacher's mediating role.

Many teachers are also guided in thinking about and selecting the subject matter by way of their own engagement in some practice, activity, or field of study. Being deeply interested in children's literature, for example, will surely impact the way a teacher conceives of the language arts and literacy as subject matter. Or think of a music teacher with an infectious passion for performing who isn't content to merely follow the standard curriculum. A teacher's sense of what some subject matter can mean is enlarged by the traditions of activity and practice in which they take part. Their way of selecting the subject matter is motivated by the desire to preserve and extend the practice and enrich the lives of students through their active engagement and vivid sense of its distinctive qualities and traditions.

For most teachers, a compromise must be struck between remaining true to their own commitments and beliefs about what is of value and meeting the expectations of external influences that bear upon the subject matter they teach. In making sense of subject matter, then, teachers attend both to externally generated conceptions of what the official curriculum consists of and to their own experiential awareness of the kinds of meaning and promise the subject matter has for them.

In broad terms, this aspect of a teacher's task boils down to this: how do they see the subject matter they will teach, even in a small way, contributing to their students' lives within the evolving traditions and practices of contemporary culture? What meaning and use might it have for them? This work places teachers, as mediators, squarely in the currents of cultural change, the ongoing story of how all kinds of traditions of learning, forms of activity, and practices rise, adapt, and evolve over time. "Basically," writes Arendt, "we are always educating for a world that is or is becoming out of joint, for this is the basic human situation, in which the world is created by mortal hands to serve mortals for a limited time as home."[9] In their ways of understanding the subject matter they are responsible for, teachers weigh in on this process. The question then becomes one of interpretation, what will we make of the subject matter. That is, the teacher is faced with an interpretive task.

Helping Students Make Sense of Subject Matter

However teachers understand their role with respect to what they *intend* to impart as subject matter, they must grapple with how to *act* on that intent. Turning now toward their students, the issue becomes how are *they*, the students, to make sense of the subject matter. Of course, that becomes a matter of interpretation for the teacher as well, in his or her mediating role. The questions are ever-present. For whom and in what way is the curriculum relevant? What is the best way to impart the material for deeper understanding? What aspects of the curriculum will require special attention? Finally, how will the subject matter impact *these* students or *this* class?

Perhaps *the* central question every teacher faces is how and in what ways the subject matter in fact matters to their particular students. The poignancy of this question for the teacher is entirely dependent on what they themselves make of the subject matter, its meaning and significance. A shallow understanding of why the content matters, on the teacher's part, yields a shallow concern for how the students engage with that content. On the other hand, teachers who find real meaning in what they teach will have a heightened interest in how their students "get it" (even if the teacher struggles to ascertain what it is the students "get"). The question—What is it to *them*?—is not always, or even very often, clearly answered. An excellent student can appear to grasp and appreciate subject matter effortlessly, and yet develop little understanding of its value. Then there is the example of Stoner, in the vignette. One question—"What does he say to you?"—is all it took for

---

[9]   Arendt, *Between Past and Future*, 192.

this seemingly dull and unremarkable student to embark upon a life enriched by literature. One simply doesn't know what students will do with and make of the subject matter they encounter. Ultimately, whatever the teacher's role in helping them, students must make sense of it on their own.

The same is true with everything students come to understand that is not explicitly part of the subject matter. What scholars call the hidden curriculum can in fact surpass the official curriculum in scope and impact.[10] You might think you are teaching quadratic equations but your students are also learning something about you and your relationship with them (your biases, quirks, virtues, etc.), about themselves (coping with boredom, addressing failure, cooperating with others, etc.), and any number of beneficial and harmful messages embedded in the organizational features of schooling (patterns of compliance, various rituals of schooling, the systematic categorization and stratification of students and their learning).

In making sense of the subject matter *both* teacher and student are thus faced with a fundamental interpretative task. Whatever traditions of learning, forms of activity, and practices are to be passed down from teacher to student, the subject matter must, in the end, be understood anew. The task of imparting the subject matter is therefore not merely one of information transfer. It doesn't take place in the same way we transfer data from our old computer to the new computer. Students are not machines that process information in a predictable, uniform fashion. To fully appreciate the role the subject matter plays in teaching, it is not enough to say what the subject matter consists of, or how we should select it; if it truly matters, we must dig deeper to understand what is involved in *how the subject matter is understood*. To help us do that, let us turn to a prominent account of understanding and its many complications. Given the complexity of human understanding and its

---

[10] Philip Jackson coined this term in *Life in Classrooms* (New York: Teachers College Press, 1990).

profound educational significance, there are a number of important features of understanding to explore in detail.

Thinking about Understanding

The most comprehensive treatment of interpretation and understanding—also called *hermeneutics*—is found in the work of Hans-Georg Gadamer. His account can shed light on how both the teacher and student make sense of the subject matter.[11] In a nutshell, Gadamer's account of understanding and its implications for teaching can be broken down into four claims:

1. *Students (and teachers) always bring their own background to bear in understanding the subject matter and everything else they encounter in life.*
2. *Their understanding proceeds in a circular fashion.*
3. *Their understanding of the world and the subject matter is intimately connected to their own self-understanding.*
4. *Their understanding is never complete.*

Let's unpack this point by point.

Students and teachers always bring their own background to bear in understanding the subject matter and everything else they encounter in life. According to Gadamer, all human understanding is historically and linguistically conditioned. We can only understand things in the world through a framework of biases, prejudgments, generalities, and traditions that we acquire from our own past experiences and the language that we have inherited to organize and make sense of our

---

[11] In this section, we draw from an earlier work on Gadamerian hermeneutics, see Dini Metro-Roland, "Hip Hop Hermeneutics and Multicultural Education: A Theory of Cross-Cultural Understanding," *Educational Studies.* 46, no. 6 (2010): 560–78. To go directly to the source, see Hans-Georg Gadamer, *Truth and Method,* 2nd edn. (New York: Bloomsbury Academic, 2013 [1975]).

experiences. Whether you are listening to a Shakespearean sonnet or a rap song, or talking with a stranger or a good friend, you always draw from your own background of past experiences to frame what you understand. Gadamer calls this framework one's *horizon of understanding.*

Each horizon of understanding is simultaneously limiting and productive. It is limiting because it is based on only one person's limited experience living in a particular time and place; but it is also productive in that human understanding isn't possible without a horizon of understanding with which to contextualize what we experience.[12] Each student (as well as the teacher) must see the world from some vantage point—*their own.*

Horizons are not static; they constantly change and expand as we chalk up new experiences in our daily life. Teaching, in fact, depends on our capacity to change. As mediators, teachers draw from their own rich experience with the subject matter to create lessons designed to broaden their students' understanding of the subject matter and its wider significance. But it isn't only our horizons of understanding that expand and change over time, so does the meaning of *what* we understand. Cultural traditions and practices are themselves dynamic and ever-changing; they shift in meaning and significance as they are understood anew and applied to an evolving historical context. Notice here the affinity between this view and Arendt's claim that in order for cultural traditions and practices to survive, they must be renewed by each new generation in novel and unforeseeable ways.

This complicates how we understand the subject matter and its significance to students. The cave paintings in Lascaux cannot have the same significance today as they did 20,000 years ago. Not only have traditions of painting changed but so have the sensibilities of the interpreters and the context in which these paintings are understood. It isn't that we can't try to see the painting as the original creators did

---

[12] Gadamer, *Truth and Method,* 245.

or understand Shakespeare's sonnets as his Elizabethan contemporaries once did, but our attempts to do so can only be at best partially successful. Your horizon of understanding will always both possess *and* lack something that theirs did not. And yet, there is generally enough overlap and flexibility in language that communication is possible even across great distances of time and space. If you stop and think about it, this is truly extraordinary. That Dr. Sloane even bothers to pose the question—*Mr. Shakespeare speaks to you across three hundred years, Mr. Stoner; do you hear him?*—is testament to the unique capacities of human language and understanding.

Despite these remarkable achievements in understanding, the central role played by our experiences is troubling. If we can only understand the world through our own horizon of understanding, then how does anyone understand something new, or even differently? Gadamer's answer to this question is found in the structure of understanding itself.

Student and teacher understanding proceeds in a circular fashion. Any time we encounter anything, be it an event, person, or thing, we enter it with prior assumptions. That is, we project an anticipated whole of what we expect to find that frames what we encounter in a recognizable context. As we proceed, these prior assumptions will have to be checked and revised against new emerging particulars if we want to gain a better understanding. Generally, our horizon of understanding of whatever it is we encounter is up to the task. It provides us with a more or less accurate framework that helps us navigate through our life without much effort. Along the way we acquire new knowledge and experience that further enriches and broadens our horizon of understanding. This is the basic circle of understanding at work—we start with an initial conception of the whole (our prior assumptions if you will) and revise our conception in light of new emerging particulars that add something new to our picture. As our conception of the whole changes, so does the significance of each of the particulars.

We most clearly feel the need for understanding precisely when our prior assumptions fail us, when our expectations hit a brick wall. If, for instance, I am confident I know how to solve an algebraic equation but then fail to do so, I am forced to reevaluate my initial judgments if I want to understand the problem better. I might decide to return to the problem or ask for advice. To successfully understand the equation, I will need to loosen the hold of some of my prior assumptions—what I think I know about the equation—and allow the truths of the problem to do their work. Only then will successful understanding be possible.

This process becomes thornier and much harder to evaluate when the subject matter is not as clear-cut as algebra. But the same general approach applies. To find a better fit between a student's own prior assumptions and what she hopes to understand better, the student must encounter the subject matter with an open and charitable frame of mind, recognizing that she has something to learn from it. Whether a student is reading a particularly difficult text, conversing with a foreign guest, or listening to someone read an abstract poem, the task is the same: to allow her initial assumptions to enter into a give-and-take encounter with another (perhaps better or at least different) perspective on the subject matter. This perspective will then be incorporated into a new and broadened horizon of understanding. In order to become truly knowledgeable in any subject matter, a student's understanding will have to undergo a long series of continual projecting and revising that often progresses in fits and starts as she faces and overcomes challenges. The student's expertise grows as her inadequate, unfruitful prejudgments are replaced by more suitable ones and a denser and richer horizon of understanding is acquired.

As mediators, teachers have a role to play in guiding students through this process. Teachers can provide students with ample opportunities for these encounters to take place. They can even enrich the process by sharing their own (more experienced and insightful) understanding of the subject matter. But teachers can't undergo this process for their students. In fact, no one can force someone to subject their prior assumptions to what the subject matter or anything else has to say. Many of us in fact are content to only hear what our own prejudgments (prejudices) tell us. We may not care to broaden our horizon of understanding at all. It is quite common for both students and teachers to cling to beliefs that reinforce their own self-image and other cherished ideas about the world. Understanding, it turns out, always entails risk that not everyone is willing to take. Why this is so has something to do with the connection between what we understand and who we are.

A student's (or teacher's) understanding of the world and the subject matter is intimately connected to self-understanding. Gadamer believes that we understand ourselves through our understanding of the world. Not only does our horizon serve as the background context for understanding things in the world (and constructing the very standards for judging these things) but, in any given situation, it also provides us with (and limits) our existential possibilities, or what William James calls a "living option" in life.[13] Being a cellist, lion-tamer, or surgeon are not really live options for me, not just because I lack the prerequisite talents to excel at them but because (so far) my horizon of understanding does not make room for such identities. I don't have any real experience with any of them. My exposure to stories and popular shows about cellists, lion-tamers, and surgeons might give me a vague notion of what it might be like to be one of these things, but not enough to be these things convincingly or to carry it out in real life. What *I am* and *can be* is largely a product of what I understand and can do with that understanding.

This apparent limitation of our understanding can be usefully reimagined by teachers as untapped potential. The uniqueness of human understanding is such that the initiation into various traditions opens up new worlds and forms of self-expression. Charles Taylor distinguishes two ways in which the subject matter (organized in language) might disclose new possibilities to us. The first, which he calls *the accessible*, allows us to be more reflectively aware of what is there in our environment. As we accrue new knowledge about the world, we

---

[13] See William James, "The Will to Believe," in *William James: Writings 1878–1899: Psychology, Briefer Course / The Will to Believe / Talks to Teachers and Students / Essays*, ed. Gerald E. Myers (New York: Library of America, 1992).

become better able to understand and navigate it. The second, which he terms *the existential,* discloses new human meanings and ways of being for us.[14] We see this latter function with young children as certain experiences in and outside of the classroom give rise to dreams about future careers as an artist one day or a soccer player another. The experience of studying abroad and other rich multicultural encounters can have similar effects on both fronts, heightening our sensitivity to the world and its possibilities, upending our prior assumptions and impelling a dramatic reassessment of our life and aspirations.

Gadamer's and Taylor's accounts illustrate how making sense of the subject matter is intimately connected to the formation of identity. That is, the way in which students understand *what* the subject matter is, *how* it works, and *why* it matters has ethical and existential implications in line with McClintock's notion of formative justice (described in Chapter 1). Adding additional complexity to these high stakes is the partial nature of human understanding itself.

Understanding is never complete. Because we don't live forever, our understanding of the world is only partial. There is always something that falls outside our horizon. The same is true of traditions which possess their own horizons that deepen and expand in the process of being understood and applied in ever-changing contexts. Dr. Sloane's interpretation of Shakespeare's sonnet, however subtle and perceptive it may be, is certainly not the last word.

"In ordinary experience," writes Northrop Frye, "we are all in the position of a dog in a library, surrounded by a world of meaning in plain sight that we don't even know is there."[15] What distinguishes an expert from a beginner, a teacher from her student, is not complete mastery of a tradition, but a denser, more intricate interpretive framework from which to make intelligible the world of meaning in our environment.

---

[14] Charles Taylor, *The Language Animal: The Full Shape of the Human Linguistic Capacity* (Cambridge: Harvard University Press, 2016), 46.

[15] Quoted in Chris Higgins, *The Good Life of Teaching: An Ethics of Professional Practice* (Oxford: Wiley Blackwell, 2011), 133.

Years of experience may help the master carpenter see the wood and its possibilities more fully than the novice, but she also knows that there are always more vantage points that lie ahead.

In many ways, Gadamer's theory of understanding raises just as many questions as answers. It neither provides a formula for imparting the subject matter nor does it necessarily diverge from traditional approaches to teaching subject matter. In fact, the classical approach of starting with complex material, breaking it down into manageable parts, and presenting it in a clear and efficient manner is still a reasonable strategy for many teaching situations. At the same time, Gadamer's theory of understanding does complicate any simplistic picture one might have of how the subject matter is imparted and what it means. It also helps us to see certain problems that warrant closer attention.

Problems of Subject Matter

All subject matter raises questions about what it means and why it matters from the point of view of the individuals making sense of or being subject to it. Such questions point to basic issues of power and authority in curriculum; subject matter can be empowering, but it is often experienced as an imposition.

In contexts where a narrow, fixed view of subject matter is imposed, everyone involved risks being cut off from vital aspects of the ongoing traditions of learning and activity that might otherwise have a powerful impact on their lives. For good or ill, the interpretive task of teaching plays a pivotal role in such prospects; all subject matter draws from the past and points toward some future, but it also must take root in the present, where teachers and students gather together to make sense of what they encounter.

Gadamer's way of thinking about understanding calls attention to key issues. It highlights the fact that each person brings something different to the table where subject matter is concerned. Teachers who fail to take this fact fully into consideration limit the way students create vital connections to the subject matter, something critical with respect to the flourishing of each student and the cultural traditions and practices being understood. Furthermore, thinking about the general characteristics of understanding—that we only understand the world through our own horizon of understanding, and that every act of understanding is unique and may have far-reaching or even transformative force—raises additional considerations for teachers. Mirroring the range of authority effects noted in Chapter 2, subject matter can evoke in student responses everything from awakened reverence to compliant attention for the sake of getting along, to varieties of resistance or rejection.

In some settings of teaching, the imposition of subject matter can do obvious harm. James Baldwin, for example, described the experience of alienated African American children who run "the risk of becoming schizophrenic" when confronted with the contradictions between their lived experience and the official history they learn in schools.[16] More recent accounts from scholars explore how efforts to "broaden the horizon" of students outside the dominant culture can become a kind of enforced cultural assimilation, denigrating other ways of life.

Proponents of culturally responsive teaching call on us to not only take into consideration a student's background in determining *how* to address the subject matter but also include such information in decisions about *what* to teach.[17] The degree to which teachers should respect what a student values and considers worthy of learning is a persistent, thorny problem. Scholars have made a living studying the ways in which unintentional collateral learning and the hidden curriculum affect student learning. The questions of who decides what subject matter is of most worth and how subject matter is understood and approached

---

[16] Baldwin, *Baldwin: Collected Essays*, 678.

[17] For one example of culturally responsive teaching, see Django Paris and H. Samy Alim, eds., *Culturally Sustaining Pedagogies: Teaching and Learning for Justice in a Changing World* (New York: Teachers College Press, 2017).

are legitimate concerns of parents, citizens, experts, teachers, and students. Those who worry that their own traditions and ideals are not adequately protected or cultivated have gone so far as to challenge the qualification of teachers and the legitimacy of their authority on the basis of their own narrow commitments and understanding.

Gadamer's hermeneutic theory complicates this picture. In terms of making sense of the subject matter, there is no such thing as a bias-free approach; prejudgments (biases, generalizations, prejudice) make up an essential part of everyone's understanding of the world. It is only a small step from there to wonder what then is to prevent our prejudgments from functioning like prejudices, thus dominating and distorting our understanding of the subject matter and imposing our understanding onto others. This could lead one to further suspect that all teacher efforts to shape the understanding of subject matter are an exercise of power of some kind, ways of seeing to it that one's students conform to and reconfirm the teacher's own biases and prejudgments. This can and does happen.

It is true that our prejudgments are never completely transparent to us. Like language, they most often work unconsciously, and we aren't clearly attuned to how they work. Theories of implicit bias refer to this tendency with respect to racial and gender discrimination. However, Gadamer's work also reminds us that we can, with effort, learn to recognize and work to overcome patterns of harmful prejudice with greater exposure to and understanding of other perspectives if we are so inclined. What teachers cannot do is get out of their skin and view the world from a neutral or purely objective standpoint. That is impossible.

Thinking carefully about the issues involved in making sense of subject matter puts this central element of a teacher's work in perspective as the deeply human form of activity that it is. And that points to the social and political dimensions of a teacher's work. At any given time, the views that prevail about subject matter—its defining boundaries, key works, principal methods, essential skills, core standards, and so on— have a profound effect on what there is to understand, an institutional bias. That Shakespeare "spoke" to Stoner and set him on the path to becoming a professor could have gone otherwise had he been assigned something else to read, or found himself in a different context in which to make sense of it. The point is that the power to establish subject matter, what counts as knowledge in any field of study, makes every student's receptivity and willingness to go on a potentially fateful thing. Often professional standards or state requirements impose a view of what counts, deciding whether Haydn or hip-hop more closely aligns, or how they might coexist, with the aims of music education a teacher advances. But this is also true where teachers represent some conception of what matters most, and is perhaps even canonical or paradigmatic, in the subject matter they impart.

A teacher's role in presenting and making sense of subject matter thus takes place in a context of power, the capacity to determine the focus and content of instruction. In recent decades, this context of power has become more prominent. Teachers working in the institution of schooling are deeply implicated in an increasingly interconnected network of activity that determines, to a great extent, how educational opportunities are distributed, who wins and who loses. Powers associated with subject matter, what it includes, who and what it encourages, and who it excludes or serves to diminish, are woven into the work of teachers. It is therefore not surprising that Gadamer's rich analysis of understanding is sometimes overshadowed by views of school learning that concentrate more attention on such questions of power. Michel Foucault, for example, coined the term "power/knowledge" to convey the ways in which power and knowledge are thoroughly intertwined and baked into institutional structures of organized expertise and control.[18] On this view, the authority of teachers as the purveyors of official knowledge is bound up in a system of power relations over which they have little control. Power and knowledge thereby converge to forge persons in the crucible of institutional surveillance, categorization, and the normalizing power of the system.

---

[18] For a treatment of Foucault and his educational implications, see Dini Metro-Roland, "Knowledge, Power, and Care of the Self," in *Beyond Critique: Exploring Critical Social Theories and Education*, eds. Barry Levinson et al. (New York: Paradigm Publishers, 2011), 139–70.

If that is true, the importance of the interpretive task we have emphasized as a key element of teaching may exaggerate the capacity of teachers to make sense of the subject matter in ways that truly make a difference for their students. Wherever you may fall in these debates, a healthy skepticism about the way subject matter is defined and approached is warranted. At the very least, the authority of teachers— their legitimate power—in interpreting *what* the subject matter is, *how* it works, and *why* it matters should be exercised with humility. What is clear, however, is that subject matter expertise is not simply mastery of some tradition of practice or field of study. It is better understood as a deeper and more fine-grained sensitivity to what the tradition or field has to offer. By this account, teachers should bring a rich and expansive horizon of understanding to bear upon what they teach while also being humbly aware of what the subject matter means in the lives of those they teach.

Why Subject Matter Matters

Subject matter is a central concern of all teachers. What it is, how it is defined, and the kinds of meaning to be made of it are, however, all matters that are open to interpretation. Making sense of subject matter is therefore an elemental concern of teachers. In that regard, we have presented a theory of understanding to suggest how it comes about that diverse activities of thought and practice, the contents of subject matter, are passed down to and in turn renewed by students over time. Teachers play a vital role by way of the actions they take in striving to impart the subject matter to their students.

Our contention is that the efforts of teachers to engage students in making sense of subject matter are more complex and meaningful than standard views of the "transmission of knowledge and information" typically suggest. Theories that reduce this process to simple information transfer fail to appreciate the full richness of the subject matter and the range of its effects. Such thinking fundamentally misunderstands the complex ways in which meaning and understanding emerge in the unfolding relationships between teachers, students, and subject matter. However we judge their merits, such relationships are powerful influences on the way one understands crucial features of our world.

Thinking about your own experience teaching and being taught

- What are the ways teachers have broadened your understanding of and appreciation for particular domains of subject matter?
- Can you identify ways teachers have hampered or undermined your capacity to make sense of some subject matter?

Thinking about conceptions and theories of subject matter in teaching

- What does understanding the subject matter entail? Is it primarily a matter of information transfer or does a theory of understanding such as Gadamer's provide a more compelling account of what takes place?
- How should we make sense of teacher expertise, the inevitable biases in understanding, and the relationship between knowledge and power in teaching?
- Can you identify ways in which your horizons of understanding have shifted on account of work with teachers?

Thinking about how subject matter relates to the other elements

- How do teacher virtues and cares come into play where subject matter is concerned?
- How do authority effects impact, whether positively or negatively, the ways in which subject matter is understood?

Thinking about subject matter in other contexts of life

- How important in life are one's capacities to encounter and make sense of matters that challenge one's understanding?
- How well does, or might, encounters with school subject matter help someone today navigate today's information society and social media?

5

Rendering Judgment

*It wasn't EVEN HALLOWEEN yet, but Ms. Hempel was already thinking about her anecdotals. The word, with all its expectations of intimacy and specificity, bothered her: a noun in the guise of an adjective, an obfuscation of the fact that twice a year she had to produce eighty-two of these ineluctable **things**. Not reports, like those written by other teachers at other schools, but anecdotals: loving and detailed accounts of a student's progress, enlivened by descriptions of the child offering a piercing insight or aiding a struggling classmate or challenging authority. It was a terrible responsibility: to render, in a recognizable way, something as ineffable as another human being, particularly a young one . . .*

"First impressions?" she asked, perched atop her desk, her legs swinging. "What do you think?"

The seventh graders looked at each other uneasily . . .

"Do you like it?" Ms. Hempel tried again. She smiled entreatingly; her shoes banged against her desk. Teaching she now understood, was a form of extortion; you were forever trying to extract from your students something they didn't want to part with: their attention, their labor, their trust.

David D'Sousa, ladies' man, came to her assistance. . . . He walked down the hallways with the rolling, lopsided gait of the rappers he so fervently admired. In the classroom his poise deserted him; he sputtered a lot, rarely delivering coherent sentences . . .

*But David was a gentleman, and ready to sacrifice his own dignity in order to rescue Ms. Hempel's. Cooperative and responsive, she thought. **Willing to take risks.***

"It's like . . .," he began, and stopped. Ms. Hempel smiled at him, nodding furiously, as if pumping the gas pedal on a car that wouldn't start. "It's . . . " He grabbed his upper lip with his bottom teeth. He ground

*his palm into the desk. The other kids delicately averted their eyes.... "It's
. . . different from the other stuff I've read in school."*

*The class exhaled: yes, it was different. They spoke about it as if they
didn't quite trust it . . .*

*"It doesn't really sound like a book," said Emily Radinsky, capricious
child, aspiring trapeze artist, lover of Marc Chagall. Ms. Hempel would
write, **Gifted**.*

*"I normally don't like books," said Henry Woo, sad sack, hanger-on,
misplacer of entire backpacks. Ms. Hempel would write, **Has difficulty
concentrating**.*

*"It's okay for us to be reading this?" said Simon Grosse, who needed to
ask permission for everything. Ms. Hempel would write, **Conscientious**.*

Sarah Shun-Lirn Bynum, *Ms. Hempel Chronicles*[1]

Ms. Hempel is portrayed in this novel as the kind of teacher who
grades pop quizzes while watching TV and detests the daily grind of
"taking attendance, enforcing detention, and making them love you."[2]
But like every teacher, she cannot escape the weighty responsibility of
rendering judgments "of intimacy and specificity" about her students.[3]
These judgments are not just institutional reports and standardized
assessments; they are attempts to get a handle on the inherent
complexity of a teacher's world.

This world is vast. Today's miracles of digital content delivery may
be designed to adapt to the emergent needs of each student, but their
range of responsiveness cannot yet replicate the sheer magnitude and
complexity of concerns that teachers routinely attend to even in the
seemingly simple act of leading a class discussion. It matters that Jalen
is not fully present today, that it is raining outside, that Ashley has just
lost her grandmother, that one's throat is sore from speaking so much,
that the students have missed a critical point not directly addressed
in the curriculum, and that Anita has never before engaged in class

---

[1]   Sarah Shun-Lirn Bynum, *Ms. Hempel Chronicles* (Boston: Mariner Books, 2009), 23–27.

[2]   Bynum, *Ms. Hempel Chronicles*, 10.

[3]   Bynum, *Ms. Hempel Chronicles*, 23.

conversation with such zeal. Responses to these and other concerns are not mere appendages to teaching, something applied after-the-fact in assessing student progress or the quality of instruction; they are *implicit* in almost everything teachers do as teachers.

Judgment, the ability to read a situation and discern what needs to be done, is an unrelenting and multifaceted feature of teaching. This is due to the inherently complex social nature of a teacher's work. The responsibilities of teachers include giving attention to a shifting array of considerations that bear upon their decision-making in practice, especially with respect to student engagement, interaction, conduct, and performance over time. Where teaching is concerned, judgment is at the center of practice, even when the choice is to hold back and let students operate on their own for a time.

A teacher's judgment, bound up as it is to her own character, cares and relationships with students, is infused with subjectivity. This is troubling to those who expect teachers to perform their duties with strict impartiality and technical know-how. We take for granted that teachers are not here to be parents or friends, but to instruct and render clear-eyed assessments about what students need and how they perform. But this is much easier said than done. For to respond well over time in practice, teachers must accurately read the specific social landscape and keep in mind all relevant evidence bearing upon their decision-making, including their own assumptions and inferences about the emerging beliefs, attitudes, perspectives, and capabilities of their students.

In this chapter, we explain why the demands of daily judgment in teaching require more than technical mastery. Teachers must also exhibit, so far as possible, *practical wisdom*, a form of discernment and action that entails a sensitivity to social context and reveals something about the character of the teacher, the stance of the students, and the demands of the situation in which she finds herself. Given the importance of judgment in teaching, we then take up issues that arise in evaluating the impact of such judgment. This includes managerial efforts to standardize forms of assessment in practice, issues regarding the subjectivity of teacher judgment, and considerations about the reciprocal nature of judgment in teaching. That is, as teachers evaluate students and their performance, they and their performance are also evaluated. As an element of teaching, judgment is both vital and contentious.

Judgment, Technical Rationality, and Practical Wisdom

Although not always recognized as such, teaching surely ranks high on any reasonable scale of demanding occupations, and indeed professions. Consider for a moment just how remarkably judgment-intensive the work of teachers is. Every element of teaching discussed in this book necessitates judgment, the *ability to anticipate or read a situation and discern both what is going on and how one should respond* at each moment. There is no avoiding judgments about how best to clarify and act upon one's central cares as a teacher; to exercise authority in ways that bring about positive effects; to respond to various situations by modeling one's own qualities of character in order to develop similar qualities in students; to understand and help students make sense of the subject matter; and to monitor student responses and performance. As we will see going forward, judgment is also essential in how teachers frame student activity and learning in terms of certain purposes, establish a setting conducive to one's conception of the work, and engage meaningfully over time with those one encounters in practice.

Moreover, the necessary kinds of judgment are for most teachers strikingly demanding in a number of ways. The sheer volume and variety of decisions governing what one does and how one responds is imposing, from monitoring student behavior, cultivating intellectual virtues, and scaffolding student understanding. The complexity of judgments called for by the nature of the work is also daunting as one judgment impinges on others. For instance, a teacher's decision to act upon certain deep cares will often affect her judgments about the curriculum and the intent of her interactions with students. And then there is the range of potential impacts of judgment, notable for example in the way teacher assessments of student work can in some instances inspire and in others extinguish passion for and engagement in some field of study.

Finally, it is worth noting that teacher judgments are spread across three interconnected time frames. Before setting foot in the classroom, teachers must render judgments in anticipating and planning for what they will do and what might unfold. Then, in the presence of students, their judgment accelerates in reaction to new developments as they emerge in practice. Finally, teachers must respond to student work, dwell on particular things that took place and adjust their teaching going forward. The work of teacher judgment is never done.

Teachers are not unique in this regard. Judgment is a universal capacity of active members of any community. Aristotle argues that it is our ability to make judgments about the world *and* to act on them that makes us ethical beings.[4] Rather than merely react to the immediate pressures and possibilities of the physical environment—as he believed other animals do—we have the power of reflection, the ability to think critically about our own situation, to weigh different scenarios, to consider ethical ramifications, and ultimately to judge how best to act and act accordingly, even when doing so conflicts with our immediate wants and desires.[5]

What makes humans ethical, in other words, is our capacity for free choice. In any situation, we could conceivably judge and act differently than we do. Our choices can be poor or wise, and often it is hard to say.

---

[4] This is of course assuming that we have free will, a question that is still hotly contested. But as P. F. Strawson and others have pointed out, even in a deterministic world void of any free will, humans can't possibly function together without holding people accountable for their actions. This is especially true for the practice of teaching. P. F. Strawson, "Freedom and Resentment," in *Freedom and Resentment, and Other Essays* (New York: Routledge, 2015 [1974]).

[5] It is because of this human capacity that Arendt calls acting without thinking an evil, see Hannah Arendt, *Eichmann in Jerusalem: A Report on the Banality of Evil* (New York: Penguin Classics, 2006 [1963]).

We generally attribute good judgment to people who consistently make wise choices in how they read and react to the environment. The clarity with which we can distinguish better and worse judgment in teaching depends in part on the nature of the subject matter. In mathematics, one can say with some conviction how one should respond to the problem 2+2 or determine the angles of an isosceles triangle. But when our choices concern human interaction—as teaching always does—there is often no clear blueprint for right judgment and right action. We lack a foolproof algorithm or lesson plan for interacting with other human beings, because each human being and each social context is unique.

According to Aristotle, to consistently judge and act well (or virtuously) in the unique and shifting circumstances of social life demands more from us than technical rationality or the ability to follow certain rules or technical procedures in bringing about predetermined results. The unique demands of social situations require a different kind of awareness, what Aristotle refers to as practical wisdom (*phronesis*). Aristotle differentiates technical skill from practical wisdom as the difference between making (*poiesis*) well and acting (*praxis*) well.[6] Teaching makes demands of both kinds. Let's consider each in turn.

We generally approach *making* things with technical rationality and sound technique. Our skill and dexterity are displayed when we reproduce things according to a blueprint. A carpenter starts with a limited supply of raw materials, forms an idea of the final product, and with the help of woodworking tools, fashions a table or chair. Technical mastery is thus exhibited in the product's likeness to the guiding idea. There is a clear path from intention to end-result and determining success is a relatively straightforward affair. Teaching is often treated this way. Popular authors, such as Doug Lemov, claim that one can "Teach like a Champion" by applying general techniques and "best

---

[6] Aristotle, *Nicomachean Ethics* (Oxford: Oxford University Press, 2009). For a more thorough account of Aristotle's notions of technical skill and practical wisdom and one that complicates this distinction more than we do here, see Joseph Dunne, *Back to the Rough Ground: Practical Judgment and the Lure of Technique* (South Bend: University of Notre Dame, 2001).

practices" to any classroom situation.[7] A teacher's technical mastery is thereby demonstrated when she manipulates the learning environment in ways that consistently meet the objectives and goals laid out in her lesson plans and in the official curriculum.

A distinctive feature of making is the detachability of parts. The final product can be easily separated from the making and the maker. That is, a third person can evaluate the product (and its craftsmanship) without any prior knowledge of who created it or the situation in which it was created. Moreover, our assessment of the maker's work reveals nothing about the moral character of the maker. You can be a good carpenter without being a good person. This objective quality renders the end product amenable to measurement. Someone viewing teaching in this technical way can design evaluation systems that assess the quality of teachers without needing to know anything about what has taken place in the classroom. The outcome of teaching in the form of a test score is thereby detached from the act of teaching itself and the teacher's moral character. Breaking down teaching into detachable parts in this way (teacher, technical skills, product, value) reduces teaching to its instrumental usefulness—it reinforces the idea that we engage in teaching *in order to* produce a predetermined endproduct. No value is afforded to the act of teaching itself or to the teacher herself outside of the specific results produced.

At times, teaching calls for a technical approach of this kind. But teaching is not simply making; it requires something more than sound technique and clear learning objectives. Entangled in the web of human relations, teachers are called to *act* with tact. Consider, for instance, our opening vignette. Ms. Hempel has assigned *This Boy's Life,* Tobias Wolff's irreverent account of growing up poor without a father.[8] The protagonist's obscene language and his tales of adolescent delinquency and self-destruction give rise to a general mood of suspicion—the

---

[7] Doug Lemov, *Teach Like a Champion 2.0: 62 Techniques That Put Students on the Path to College* (San Francisco: Jossey-Bass, 2015).

[8] Tobias Wolff, *This Boy's Life* (New York: Grove Press, 1989).

students are uneasy about sharing their intimate feelings about such an illicit topic. Understanding this, the teacher sits casually on the desk, swinging her feet, in a deliberate attempt to connect with the students and draw out their genuine first impressions. David's initial response is tenuous and anxiety-ridden—and not just because of his fear of public speaking, but also because of the raw nature of the subject matter. His honest observation that "it . . . is different from the other stuff I've read in school" has a palpable effect on the others.[9] The tension released, students begin to share their thoughts with more bravado, revealing something about themselves and their understanding of the book's transgressive content in the process.

There is nothing extraordinary about this event; such conversations happen all the time in classrooms. What is significant and often overlooked is the rich interplay of intuitions, feelings, beliefs, and interpretations just beneath the surface as both teacher and students are called to action. The teacher must correctly discern the mood of the students as she builds rapport and raises questions just the right way while the students must overcome not only their initial hesitations and trust the space but also their ability to separate from their own understanding of the story what belongs and does not belong in a school-sanctioned conversation. The teacher holds the students to account and is herself judged in the process. All this happens within seconds and it would be hard, even in hindsight, to fully articulate what has just taken place and what has been accomplished.

Note the differences between acting—what Ms. Hempel is called to do here—and our account of making. First of all, her actions are inherently social; they occur with and depend on other people. The interpersonal dimension of action and its moral features disrupt the simplistic means-ends dynamic of the technical teaching paradigm. Unlike making, there is no clear break between the act, the actor, and the final product. The act cannot be separated from the persons involved because part of

---

[9] Bynum, *Ms. Hempel Chronicles*, 26–27.

the point of acting resides in the disclosing of oneself to others. Rather than merely serve a predetermined instrumental purpose—the means to creating something else—action is (at least in part) its own end. That is, much more is going on in our vignette than giving a simple account of *A Boy's Life*—the text being discussed. David is brave and valiant as Ms. Hempel is relaxed and unassuming; the others express themselves as well as they come to terms with the irreverent content in a public forum. This self-referential quality—that it reflects and simultaneously forms the character of the actors—links action to understanding and the complexities of the subject matter described in Chapter 4. We aren't simply transferring information here, and there is much more going on than can be contained in a lesson plan.

In contrast to making, notice the relationship here between the actor, the means employed, and the ends being sought in action. While the actor strives for a good result, the result cannot be so easily detached from the actor's character and the unique moral features and demands of the situation. In acting, the actor reveals something about the kind of person she is and the particular social environment in which she acts. What makes teacher judgment a terrible responsibility to Ms. Hempel is the fact that she must render "in a recognizable way, something as ineffable as another human being, particularly a young one" and act accordingly. Anthony Kenny argues that it is precisely the "morally relevant features" of the field that demand something more than technical rationality and instrumental calculation.[10] His illustration that "A needs cheering up, that B is being offensive, and one is hurting C's feelings" can be added to our earlier examples that Jalen is for some reason not fully present, Ashley is obviously depressed having just lost her grandmother, Anita has never before engaged in conversation with such zeal, and so on. Each feature in the environment demands a response that reveals not only the character of the teacher as caring, responsible, prejudiced, serious, prudent, officious, and so on but also

---

[10] Quoted in Dunne, *Back to the Rough Ground*, 301.

the nature of her relationship with the other actors involved. We saw this earlier in Annas' account of modeling virtue in Chapter 3. It is difficult to separate the actor from the acting and its consequences.

Because of these differences, acting requires more than sound technique. It calls for what Aristotle calls *practical wisdom*, a kind of judgment that is particularly sensitive to the unique social context when discerning what is going on and what must be done. This form of judgment also illuminates something about the kind of person one is; being practically wise displays the actor's moral character and her sensitivity to the unique moral features and demands of each situation. For Aristotle, practical wisdom is also the intellectual virtue that helps us realize our intentions in virtuous activity. Good intentions alone don't make one courageous or honest; one must discern how one is required to act in order to carry out one's good intentions in each specific context. It isn't enough for teachers to wish students well or to care about their learning. They must have the good judgment to consistently convey their care in ways that bring about good results. Note that what constitutes a good result in acting depends on each situation and is itself a matter of judgment. There is no one way that all students should turn out. Nor is consistently achieving high test scores the only measure of success. High test scores may not mean much if in the process students develop a disdain for the subject or acquire habits that undermine their interest in applying what they know.

The distinction made here between acting and making is admittedly simplistic. In practice, there is significant overlap between acting and making. Both technical skill and practical wisdom are complex and necessary in social life and teaching. Good teaching includes sound technique. It is also reasonable to consider how well students meet certain relevant standards in evaluating the effectiveness of teachers. The problem occurs when technical mastery eclipses practical wisdom in our effort to standardize and manage teaching and teachers. Not only do we distort teaching when we reduce it to technical mastery and the delivery of predetermined, measurable results but we also diminish the value of teachers when we reduce their role to effective classroom managers.

Managerial effectiveness, as Alasdair MacIntyre puts it, is the "manipulation of human beings into compliant patterns of behavior."[11] The conceit of managers, he argues, lies in the fiction that such effectiveness is in some way morally neutral. One can't exercise the "62 techniques that put students on the path to college" as Lemov's subtitle suggests teachers do, without making a series of moral judgments about students and their learning.[12] While we can certainly describe a teacher's task in these narrow technical terms, the social features of teaching cannot be so easily dismissed.

We are left then with two forms of teacher judgment—two ways to read and react to what the situations of practice demand. On the one hand, we have a technical rationality that strives to meet predetermined objectives in a consistent and efficient fashion. This requires good technique and an ability to achieve predetermined results. On the other hand, we have practical wisdom. To act well in any social situation, one must respond to the particular demands of each concrete situation. In the process of acting prudently, one also displays something of oneself and the particular social context in which one acts.

It is our view that as an element of teaching, judgment incorporates both technical mastery and practical wisdom. Good teachers often possess both a strong command of their subject matter and the skills of classroom management and delivery. It is difficult to be an effective teacher unless you know your stuff well and can consistently and efficiently carry out your plans and meet your objectives. But just as teaching the subject matter is irreducible to simple information transfer, teacher judgment entails more than the ability to execute a well-designed plan. Teachers aren't creating widgets, they are nurturing the passions and potentials of human beings. We want our students to not only learn how to read but also love reading. It is the human context of teaching that renders good judgment in teaching something more than sound technique.

[11] Alasdair MacIntyre, *After Virtue*, 3rd edn. (Notre Dame: University of Notre Dame, 2010), 74.

[12] Lemov, *Teach Like a Champion*.

The Human Context of Practical Wisdom

In practice, wise teachers are sensitive to the unique demands of the social landscape. We are not solely dealing with abstract ideas, inanimate objects, or even irrational animals. Human beings, according to a variety of rich philosophical traditions, are unique and irreplaceable. As Arendt puts it, "we are all the same, that is, human, in such a way that nobody is ever the same as anyone else who ever lived, lives, or will live."[13] Rather than constitute silent, passive objects with clear values waiting to be mined and actuated, students and the social context in which they find themselves regularly talk back, reacting to the intentions and personal force of the teacher in significant and unpredictable ways. Further complicating teaching is what might be called a *surplus of meaning*, a seemingly endless array of interpretations and actions that permeates the teaching landscape.[14] The practical wisdom needed to navigate this landscape is less like the application of law-like principles with predictable outcomes than it is the realization of an emergent moral sensibility and responsiveness to the uniqueness of each situation and its demands.

What constitutes a wise decision in any situation is far from simple. The best action (or even a good action) depends on striking the right balance. Formulas can only get you so far—which is why preservice teachers can't acquire practical wisdom through study alone and why it is almost impossible to find in digital forms of content delivery. While experienced teachers frequently make good use of technique and formulas, they must also determine, from the complex landscape of factors and considerations, the right time, right extent and right purpose of their application.

---

[13] Hannah Arendt, *The Human Condition* (Chicago: University of Chicago, 1998 [1958]), 8.

[14] For more on this, see Paul Ricoeur, *Interpretation Theory: Discourse and the Surplus of Meaning* (Fort Worth: Texas Christian University Press, 1976) or Gadamer, *Truth and Method*.

Teachers, therefore, need experience to acquire practical wisdom. According to Joseph Dunne, practical wisdom develops within the continually expanding circle of understanding, described in Chapter 4.[15] The insights guiding master teachers may not show up at all to someone who lacks their heightened sensitivity and rich horizon of understanding. No matter how knowledgeable novice teachers may be in their subject matter, they simply do not see things in their environment that experienced teachers can take for granted. Of course, the expertise of teachers and the status of their professional judgment is open to interpretation. There is little consensus about what exactly constitutes teacher expertise and whether, in many contexts of teaching at least, the judgment of some teachers is to be trusted over the judgment of others.

John Dewey goes so far as to ground the authority of the teacher in the expectation that the teacher is the most experienced person in the group.[16] By most experienced, Dewey does not mean a teacher who has lived more years or spent more time unreflectively repeating certain activities in the classroom. Veteran teachers can also consistently fail to find the right balance as they go through the motions of teaching and rely too heavily on prejudice solidified by habit. An experienced person is one who is routinely open to novel meanings and understandings, who is not afraid to question her own prejudices when facing an unfamiliar situation. Through years of deliberation, judgment and action (and many failures as well) the experienced teacher refines and deepens her horizon of understanding about her subject, her students, and her life. In doing so, she gradually casts aside standard rules of thumb, scripted routines, and other crutches indispensable to novice teachers, and learns to rely on her own judgment of what is required. It is not that she does away with general principles entirely, only that she can more intuitively and reliably

---

[15] Dunne, *Back to the Rough Ground*, 303.

[16] Dewey, *Experience and Education*, 58–59.

trust her experience to apply general principles appropriately to each unique and concrete case.[17]

There are no magic formulas to quicken the process of acquiring practical wisdom. Teacher education programs, no matter how well designed, cannot deliver good teacher judgment on their own. Teachers must develop practical wisdom by exercising judgment in practice. The conditions are similar to those laid out in Chapters 2 and 4: teachers need exposure, practice, and the aspiration both to learn from experience and to attain high ideals. Reforms that severely restrict teacher judgment may bring about short-term uniformity and a burst of productivity, but they can also delay the cultivation of practically wise teachers whose judgments are indispensable for the successful operation of schools and serve as sources of inspiration for students and young teachers alike.

Evaluating the Impact of Teacher Judgment

If teaching were entirely a matter of technical rationality, we could judge the work of teachers by what they bring about, the end product of their work. Given the scope and complexity of judgments embedded in their work, teachers know that would not do justice to what they do. Still, questions arise about how teachers, as well as other interested parties, can begin to assess and evaluate the quality of judgments that teachers must make in and about their work. How do we know when we are on the right track?

Ms. Hempel's reports are one instance of a vast array of ways that teachers judge the ongoing learning and progress of students. Assessments can range from highly subjective accounts to rigorously precise measures. Acts of assessing student performance include

---

[17] For a description of how expertise is developed, see Hubert L. Dreyfus and Stuart E. Dreyfus, "Expertise in Real World Contexts," *Organization Studies* 26, no. 5 (2005): 779–91.

informal judgments formed by way of observing student work, "formative" judgments useful for the sake of monitoring and directing efforts at improvement, or casting "summative" judgments that aim to draw conclusions about what has been accomplished. Evaluative judgments as to the worth or value of student accomplishments— whether based upon comparison to other students or some particular standard—are likewise commonplace, and have a long history.[18] At the same time, the nature of assessment has radically changed with the advent of modern schooling.

Institutional Forms of Assessment

What separates modern schooling from other contexts of teaching is less the need to assess than the nature of the assessments and the degree to which they are standardized. Since the rise of the industrial workplace, reformers have sought to apply more rigorous psychometric and management principles to the evaluation of performance, including that of schools where such principles were applied. Proponents of this view believe that if we are reliably to hold students, teachers and schools accountable, we must isolate the object of evaluation from the social and moral context of schooling. This raises the question whether standardized assessments can evaluate what is, in essence, a deeply personal and individualized process. But proponents insist that what is lost in depth of understanding when we apply standardized assessments is gained in precision and objectivity. The contention is that such instruments can reveal many things about student learning without necessarily undermining the personal quality of what is learned.

The quality of current standardized assessments and their application is hotly debated. Given the complexity of the subject matter

---

[18] In Tablet Houses from the 3rd millennium cities of Nippur, Ur, Sippar, and Kish, archaeologists have found thousands of cuneiform tablets of "remarkable uniformity and systematic completeness, written in over 500 different hands" used as exercises to train scribes so that they too can make reports. Mark Griffith, "Origins and Relations to the Near East," in *Ancient Education* (Oxford: John Wiley and Sons, 2015), 8.

discussed in Chapter 4, there is something woefully incomplete with any system of evaluation that must, in order to maintain scientific standards of validity and generalizability, reduce the subject matter to measurable information isolated from the rich social context in which it is understood. This same reductive tendency is found in methods of teacher judgment when testing drives education so thoroughly that teachers are reduced to technicians. Nor do these systems of evaluation provide us with the fine-grained analysis earned through extensive teacher-student relationships. We can tell that Juan has higher scores than Janice but not say much about why and how these relative strengths are connected to student interests, a richer understanding of the subject matter, the ability to apply one's knowledge in various contexts, and the unique circumstances in which knowledge was acquired. Beyond broad categories of race, gender, and class, these instruments are blind to the specificity of individual learners and their social situation.

A common criticism of standardized assessments is their symptomatic misapplication. Rather than highlight specific features of or gaps in education that might inform student and teacher practice, the lessons to be learned from assessments are often obscured by the simplifying logic of instrumentalism.[19] Under its spell, the point of teaching is to achieve the desired results. Learning objectives become a teacher's sole focus and all other aspects of teaching are channeled in service of their attainment. Learning the names of students, making sense of a poem, organizing an ad hoc lab experiment, or providing time for open-ended discussion are *only* valuable to the extent that they help students meet specific goals. When accountability systems carry high stakes for those involved, pressure is applied to focus upon goals that link closely to the measures being used, the bottom line of a test score.

---

[19] Instrumentalism: In this context, it is the belief that teaching is to be judged only in terms of its utility, or its instrumental value in achieving intended outcomes.

As a natural extension of this instrumentalist logic, standardized systems for assessing student learning have recently been applied to the evaluation of teachers and schools.[20] Such "value added measures," as they are called, which use student test scores to evaluate the work of others, raise a distinct issue. As Danielle Allen points out, the students being tested become "the instruments for judging something other than themselves and their own flourishing."[21] With the emergence of data-driven systems, this instrumentalist way of thinking is—by design—applied all the way down, directing teacher judgment as much as possible.

This relatively recent form of standardized assessment makes up only a small portion of teacher judgment in school settings. More common (and more significant) forms of judgment are found in the formal and informal assessments administered by teachers each day that range from the purely academic to what Ms. Hempel tries to capture in her anecdotals. A good teacher will match her assessments to the subject matter. Formal exams, pop quizzes, essays may be entirely inappropriate for some subjects, but are a mainstay for evaluating learning in others. Unless one is especially data-driven, most assessments function in personal and subtle ways, fitted to each situation: a head nod and a smile, a look of consternation, a doubling back to get clarification, a decision to work one-on-one or invite group collaboration. As with the modeling of virtue, there is a constant cycle of modeling, providing space for practice and mistakes, assessment and correction, back to modeling again. A teacher's discernment is critical here. The right balance is needed to draw out the latent capacities of those being taught.

---

[20] For an analysis of recent trends in teacher evaluation, see Linda Darling-Hammond, Audrey Amrein-Beardsley, Edward Haertel, and Jesse Rothstein, "Evaluating Teacher Evaluation," *The Phi Delta Kappan* 93, no. 6 (March 2012): 8–15.

[21] Danielle Allen, *Education and Equality* (Chicago: University of Chicago Press, 2016), 19.

The Subjective Roots of Teacher Judgment

There is something right about Ms. Hempel's discomfort with the "terrible responsibility" of the anecdotal, even beyond the fact that the formalization of these "lovely and detailed" personal accounts rarely (if ever) serves its ostensible purpose. She takes the act of judgment seriously. It is a heavy burden to judge someone "as ineffable as a human being, particularly a young one" whose self-regard and talents are still not fully developed. Still this is just what teachers must do with varying degrees of accuracy and effect. While a teacher's ability to predict whether a student will complete college may have no more predictive value than a standardized test score or the educational attainment of parents, teachers clearly see something in their students that is simply not (and cannot be) contained in formal accountability systems. Teacher judgment of more subjective kinds influences both how students are taught and the kinds of impact teachers have.

The power dynamics of this relationship magnify the impact of teacher judgment. A student's long-term interest in history or music may depend more on the teacher's appraisals about her and the subject matter than any inherent talent for or prior interest in the subject itself. In some ways, the two are inseparable in the minds of learners. As the arbiter of quality, teacher judgment has *performative force*.[22] A "C" paper is just that, mediocre, because the teacher deems it so; at some point, a student whose work is regularly judged mediocre becomes, in an important sense simply *is*, a "C student." It is the fear of such judgment that leaves the normally confident David D'Sousa sputtering before the class. To hold another human being to account— especially when one is not a parent—and to have one's decisions mean so much in a person's development is a burden that most teachers do not carry lightly.

---

[22] Performative Utterance: This is a form of speech act which not only describes reality but also changes it in some way. For instance, the effect of the utterance "I now pronounce you husband and wife" when spoken by the proper authority at a wedding.

Judgment is implicit in what teachers and students care about. It is certainly evident in the cultivation of disciplinary knowledge, skills, and virtues and it also plays a significant role in caring for others. We noted in Chapter 1 Nel Noddings' notion of caring which calls on teachers to be sensitive to the particular interests and needs of each student. McClintock's conception of formative justice (also discussed in Chapter 1) underscores the stakes involved in making judgments that may open and close doors to various opportunities or fields of study.

Such labels are often used as if they are simply descriptive, but it is not that simple. Judgments placing people in categories feed into a student's self-awareness and shape expectations going forward. Importantly, in the context of schooling especially, teacher judgments about student ability and performance may also have "looping effects" creating a self-fulfilling prophecy.[23] Take the "C student" for example. Even such a modest label of ordinariness, if it sticks, may lead him to foreclose in his own mind a whole array of possible avenues to pursue in his life. As he absorbs the sense of himself as a "C student," the looping effect would be evident in his acting the part, doing and being what "C students" tend to do and be in the school or area of study in which his ordinariness is anticipated. The effects of such looping are often insidious. The history of schooling casts a long shadow over the role that teachers have played in using deeply prejudicial categories and labels to cement and justify pernicious patterns of social-economic, racial, and ethnic stratification.[24] Even seemingly innocent labels, such as when a teacher thinks of her "strong readers" when composing reading groups of similar academic talents, may have implications with respect to the potentially fateful stratification of students.

At the same time, categorization of one kind or another may be inevitable; it is certainly commonplace in all schools. Some labels, as in

---

[23] Ian Hacking, *The Social Construction of What?* (Cambridge: First Harvard University Press, 1999).

[24] For a historical account of this, see David Tyack and Larry Cuban, *Tinkering with Utopia: A Century of Public School Reform* (Cambridge: Harvard University Press, 1995).

areas of special education, are legally mandated or at least professionally required as educational services are provided. Educators also commonly employ a host of labels, stereotypes, and euphemisms in order to manage the complexity of school organization and experience. The subjective roots of judgment and its history in schools warrant a healthy degree of skepticism about the terms and categories such judgments employ and perpetuate. But, in the end, it falls to the teacher to use good judgment in questioning and revising the terms and categories of judgment they think with and act upon in their work, and to be mindful of the impacts their judgments may have.

The Judgment of Others

It would be a mistake to say that judgment flows in only one direction. Not only is the practice of teaching built on the constant need for self-assessment but it also transpires under the gaze of others. As the title of an insightful book on schooling puts it, *The Students are Watching.*[25] Teachers are always subject to the scrutiny of students as well as that of other interested parties. Whatever the weight of institutional authority, a teacher is unlikely to get very far if her judgment is constantly called into question.

Being judged with regard to one's work in teaching does not necessarily signal a crisis in authority. It depends upon the teacher's judgment as she responds in turn. In fact, this is a natural and often beneficial feature of social life. Part of being human is that we not only have intentions and judgments about others but we also know that others are judging us. That they hold our actions to account. This intentionality is a deep part of our nature and it plays an important role in education too. Even in so-called traditional classrooms with "the sage on the stage" there is no such thing as passive learning. On some

---

[25] Theodore R. Sizer and Nancy Faust Sizer, *The Students Are Watching* (Boston: Beacon Press, 1999).

level, teachers are answerable to students as students are to teachers. Student judgment often guides instruction and a sizeable portion of a teacher's professional judgment is forged by the continual need, as Ms. Hempel so eloquently puts it, "to extract from your students something they didn't want to part with: their attention, their labor, their trust."

Problems of Judgment

We have suggested that teachers judge and act at the intersection of concerns arising from three sources. One source is the public; individuals and interest groups reflecting diverse social and political perspectives desire to know the basis of judgments made about the impact and outcomes of teaching. A concern for objective and even quantifiable evidence upon which to make public judgments about the work of teachers is commonplace. The second source of concerns is the subjectivity of teachers themselves, as they dwell upon and judge how best to manage the demands that the elements of practice thrust upon them day by day in their work. Finally, there are concerns that arise from the social context in which teacher judgment and action takes place, the pressures of acting under the watchful eyes of students, fellow teachers, administrators, parents, as well as more remote observers of what teachers do.

The reality of situated teacher judgment is thus an unstable nexus of political, personal, and social perspectives, unfolding over time. All concerns lead to the problem of human judgment. Teachers, like all of us, are prone to various errors. They routinely misjudge the social landscape, the latent capacities and strengths of their students, and the significance of the subject matter. Teachers can also act rashly based on their emotions, prejudice, and bad will. Even the best teachers make errors of judgment, misinterpreting what students need at a given moment or failing to respond to critical situations with appropriate tact and grace.

Given this, it is tempting to write off practical wisdom altogether. The spell of instrumentalism is alluring to many who harbor a nagging belief that teacher judgment is irredeemably flawed. Risk and error can therefore only be controlled, they believe, by establishing transparent, neutral, and fully integrated systems of accountability based on sound scientific principles of management. The same principles used to rigidify the subject matter alluded to in the previous chapter are applied to managing instruction and assessment. The more discretion a teacher has in her daily work, the greater is the threat to system integrity.

It may also be that practical wisdom is highly valued precisely because we so often act imprudently. There is a sense from many quarters that a great deal is riding on the practical judgment of teachers, though of course there is no real agreement about what it is that matters most. And that is the rub. The antidote to poor judgment in teaching is better judgment rather than no judgment at all, but there is no consensus on what "getting things right" would look like in each situation. Teachers shouldn't be the only ones to decide the mark of good judgment in teaching, but their voice and perspective are and should be crucial in deliberations about their work.

Why Judgment Matters

One can't sidestep human judgment in the formation of human actors. It is our contention in this chapter that teaching entails both making and acting. Practical wisdom is the virtue of acting well. It is therefore a necessary virtue of teachers who desire to address the unique demands of the social landscape, a landscape permeated with moral and existential features, and the feelings, emotions, judgments, and actions of students. As such, it is not something that can be replicated by the application of standardized rules and principles but which must be developed through years of experience.

It is also true that practical wisdom is not only a teaching virtue but also a universal virtue for any participant in a moral community. Teachers are needed, whether formal or otherwise, to model and develop students' natural powers of reflection, their ability to think critically about their situation, weigh different scenarios, consider ethical ramifications, and even act against their own immediate desires and instincts for the sake of others. After a two-year study of a high school in San Francisco, Kristina Rizga reached this same conclusion:

> Some of the most important things that matter in a quality education—critical thinking, intrinsic motivation, resilience, self-management, resourcefulness, and relationship skills—exist in the realms that can't be easily measured by statistical measures and computer algorithms, but they can be detected by teachers using human judgment.[26]

Human judgment may be flawed, but teachers have no alternative. They cannot avoid exercising judgment that bears upon those they teach, who in turn are learning lessons about what it means to judge and act in a human world.

Thinking about your own experience teaching and being taught

- Considering the full range of teacher judgment in your experience, can you recall experiences in which a teacher's judgments particularly impressed or troubled you? Why?
- What accounts for teacher judgment being pivotal in both successful and unsuccessful teaching experiences?

Thinking about conceptions and theories of judgment in teaching

- What kind of judgment is it most important for a teacher to possess? To what degree is teaching a product of technical mastery? In what way does it require practical wisdom?

---

[26] Kristina Rizga, *Mission High: One School, How Experts Tried to Fail It, and the Students and Teachers Who Made It Triumph* (New York: Nation Books, 2015), xiii.

- Is Aristotle's theory of practical wisdom convincing? Why or why not?

Thinking about how judgment relates to the other elements of teaching

- Since practical wisdom is itself a virtue in teaching, how does it relate to the way other virtues are displayed and cultivated in practice?
- What are some of the key ways that judgment enters into other elements of teaching thus far addressed?

Thinking about judgment in other contexts of life

- How well has your exposure to the exercise of judgment in teaching prepared you for thinking about and exercising good judgment in other walks of life?
- Could teachers do more, under the right conditions, to model good judgment and practical wisdom? How so and under what conditions?

6

Articulating Purpose

We begin with David Denby's account of an hour drawn from a year-long observation of a few teachers of English.

Absolute silence. Hardly a sigh or a shift in position. Twenty-three students were reading in silence, and I thought to myself, "You can't fake attentiveness—there's always some giveaway." If you weren't reading, your eyes would be elsewhere or veiled, looking inward. These teenagers were lost in books...

School had started in September. It was now May. It had taken eight months, five classes a week for Miss Zelenski, eighty minutes a class, for the students to get to this point. At the beginning of the year, most of the class had been unwilling to read at all.

They came into class with elaborate handshakes, hilarity, mimicry, hugs, studied rebuffs, then mock-accusations, quarrels over small things. Lost pencils, lost assignment sheets, who sits where. Meeting at 10:40 in Miss Zelenski's room, the students, back in September, took a considerable time to get ready. "Miss, I almost got arrested yesterday," said one boy to Miss Zelenski as he came in. A girl who had received a good grade on a class essay, asked, "Are you proud of me, a little proud?" "Yes, I'm very proud," Miss Zelenski said. A few were unprepared for class, but many others were entertaining the room, and some were lost in their cell phones and MP3 players, texting or listening to music. A few sat dead-eyed, half-asleep, and then laid their heads down on the desk and dozed. Some ate candy or cookies, and I wondered if they had eaten much for breakfast. Or if they had gotten up early to get younger brothers and sisters off to school.

*Jessica Zelenski started shouting over the noise; she shouted **through** it, into it, until the students quieted down or woke up. If she were a singer,*

Zelenski would be called a belter. She was brass-lunged, and she mixed it up with the students, demanding answers, chafing, taunting, and then offering praise, her voice changing from strident to almost caressing as she welcomed something a student said. She was five five, but her boots, her high heels, her big voice, and her way of striding around the room made her seem taller. When students didn't show up, cutting school, or hanging out in some corner of the vast building, she was angry. They had to be there, in her room.

David Denby, *Lit Up*[1]

Jessica Zelenski, a veteran English teacher, does what many teachers must do. She juggles demands thrust upon her from different angles, from the school administration, from her students, from her own professional commitments, and from the realities of the economically depressed swath of New Haven in which she works. Each pulls her in a different direction, bringing with it a new set of challenges. Ms. Zelenski faces these challenges admirably, even if this means sometimes working at cross-purposes.

The question why she teaches—*her* purpose—is complex. As it is with most teachers, purpose is multifaceted and not easily packaged in a statement of aims and objectives. Ms. Zelenski wants many things from and for her students, and she sees her teaching as full of purpose, even though her efforts might not improve the material conditions of her students' lives. In Denby's account, Ms. Zelenski is not naïve; she is clear-eyed about the stark realities facing her students. "'Don't use Sunday school lessons about kindness,' she said. 'You're almost adults. And some of what you hear about life isn't good.'"[2] There is much of life that isn't good for many of these students and moral platitudes or would-be hero teachers can do little to alter that fact. Facing long odds of ever attending college, or in some cases even finding gainful employment, Ms. Zelenski nevertheless believes that literature is

---

[1] David Denby, *Lit Up: One Reporter. Three Schools. Two-Four Books That Can Change Lives* (New York: Henry Holt, 2016), 144 and 150–51.

[2] Denby, *Lit Up*, 156.

important. "Maybe they will enjoy life more, if I can get them reading," she comments to Denby, adding that "I would like to nurture in them the idea that there are other worlds. You don't have to experience things the way you do now."[3]

As admirable, quixotic, or patronizing as this long-term justification may be, it makes up only part of Ms. Zelenski's desire to act in purposeful ways. In her daily activities, purpose is more often grounded in the exigencies of the moment. Yes, her goal is to lead them to the point in the year when they can read quietly, completely engrossed in their literary worlds, but even that aim is easily lost in the immediacy of her tasks. She yells at or flatters them to get their attention, coaxes them to engage with specific content, advises and consoles them regarding their efforts, and withholds critical judgment to establish a safe space for intellectual risk and exploration. Tactics like these are among the tools of the trade, familiar to many teachers.

The main drivers of purpose have not changed that much through the centuries. The work of teachers in all kinds of cultural and institutional contexts is tied to some conception of valued and achievable ends. These ends might range from being quite specific—cultivating certain skills and talents—to broader community interests in virtues and knowledge of a more general kind, upholding social norms, or even maintaining certain cultural boundaries and ways of life. As in Ms. Zelenski's class, purpose spans the spectrum from the specific to the general, from tackling pressing tasks to laying the foundations for larger purposes that might extend into the future.

Purpose is therefore elemental to teaching. It is intentionality with respect to purpose that distinguishes teachers from others who spontaneously teach something off the cuff as the situation demands. While we learn from others in such ways, a teacher's relationship with

---

[3] Denby, *Lit Up*, 146. For works on the value of literature, see Maxine Greene, *Releasing the Imagination: Essays on Education, the Arts and Social Change* (New York: Jossey-Bass, 1995) and Martha Nussbaum, *Cultivating Humanity: A Classical Defense of Reform in Liberal Education* (Cambridge: Harvard University Press, 1998).

her students is shaped by *enduring pedagogical intent*. Functioning at the intersection of understanding and judgment, purpose adds focus, clarity, and consistency to the nature of the relationship and what might come of it. It also anchors a teacher's understanding of the subject matter and practical judgment in a wider nexus of meaning, action, and cares.

In this chapter, we explore the various ways in which purpose is understood and acted upon in teaching. First, we examine how societal and institutional conceptions of purpose, often devised by outside stakeholders, see the work of teachers as serving broad societal aims, such as economic growth or social justice. We then investigate the kinds of purpose that emerge more directly from the work of teachers as they develop relationships and interact with their students. Teachers, we suggest, are often more engaged with developing the individual capacities and interests of their students than realizing some larger political or economic project. Because teaching is personal and relies on the complex interplay of the teacher's understanding (hermeneutic skill) and judgment (practical wisdom), what constitutes both student flourishing and teacher purpose varies enormously. We end this chapter by exploring some of the nuances and contradictions of such intentions.

Societal Goals in the Work of Teachers

There are few social, political, economic, moral, or environmental problems for which education has not been seen by some as the solution. Education, commentators suggest, can serve as an elixir for social ills ranging from unemployment to injustice as well as a main driver of economic growth and political stability.[4] Today, the rise of schooling as

---

[4]   In ancient Babylonia, schools were established to create a group of scribes who could manage the complex economic and political demands of society by recording history, keeping track of business transactions and wealth, and interpreting texts of artistic, legal, political and religious significance.

a global institution is largely based upon its presumed social utility and the various social and economic goals and purposes that schooling is intended to serve.

Justifications for public education always reflect the pursuits, priorities, fears, and hopes of the time. According to Danielle Allen, the rise of compulsory education has led to a neoliberal[5] and utilitarian[6] conception of education that closely identifies educational success with the economic growth and political stability of the nation.[7] This conception persists today in what some call the *human capital approach*, the view that students are a resource to invest in, a resource optimized by schools preparing students for careers and active participation in the global economy. We could quote any number of past and present politicians who espouse the human capital approach. Former Michigan governor and business executive, Rick Snyder, captured this view quite clearly in his special message to the Michigan legislature upon taking office:

> One of Michigan's most pressing responsibilities is ensuring that students are prepared to enter the workforce and to take advantage of new opportunities as our economy grows. Michigan's future is absolutely dependent on making our education system a success for our students, our teachers, our parents and our economy.
>
> Our education system must position our children to compete globally in a knowledge-based economy. To prepare and train the next generation of workers, Michigan needs a capable, nimble and innovative work force that can adapt to the needs of the emerging knowledge-based economy and compete with any nation.
>
> To accomplish that, Michigan's education system must be reshaped so that all students learn at high levels and are fully prepared to enter

---

[5] Neoliberal: A recent version of liberalism that emphasizes free market capitalism.

[6] Utilitarianism: When applied to governments, it is the view that we should calculate our actions and promote policies that bring about the greatest amount of Happiness (or Utility) to the greatest number of people.

[7] Allen, *Education and Equality*, 12.

> the workforce or attend college. They must think and act innovatively, demonstrate high performance, and meet the highest expectations. In addition, our students must leave high school with the skills to make sound financial decisions and demonstrate a basic understanding of personal finance.[8]

What distinguishes the human capital paradigm from others is not so much its acknowledgment of education's economic benefits but its proponents' blanket disregard for other compelling educational values and aims. Allen describes the impact of this approach in terms of a narrow utilitarian calculation. Not only is economic growth the primary justification for public education but it also serves as its guiding measure. That is, in its purest form, what students learn is only valuable to the extent that it leads to personal and collective economic success. The emphasis on college preparedness, here, has less to do with any commitment to liberal studies or creative exploration than with the realization that today's competitive global market demands a broadly educated workforce.

On the surface, the human capital paradigm offers a realistic, even persuasive, justification for investing in education. For more than a century, broad economic considerations have contributed to the rise of public schools. Proponents of this paradigm argue that the economic growth stimulated by the expansion of public education also paved the way for advances in health and technology, increased political stability, and a higher quality of life and greater freedom for its citizens. Progress in these essential areas, they suggest, will continue with the establishment of a system more efficiently geared toward career- and college-readiness, adding that the nonmaterial fruits of education depend on individual tastes that are best cultivated alongside a strong and well-functioning economy. Moreover, the explicit instrumentalism of this approach—that we educate others, or indeed that we educate

---

[8] Rick Snyder, *Special Message from Governor Rick Snyder: Educational Reform* (Lansing, MI: Michigan Legislature, April 27, 2011).

ourselves, in order to produce clear economic benefits—is, to many observers, both simple to understand and compelling.

The human capital paradigm is not without its detractors, however. Critics object to the practice of treating students as human resources to be manipulated in predictable ways for the benefit of a strong economy. Some go so far as to argue that no amount of collective benefit can justify reducing free and rational human beings (persons who deserve to be recognized as ends-in-themselves) to mere cogs in a system. In normal commercial relations, parties on both sides ideally participate in a mutually beneficial exchange—for example, we voluntarily go to dentists to clean our teeth and accountants to do our taxes in exchange for the fees agreed upon. But this is not the case where the schoolwork of students is concerned. Young people in particular are not choosing to work for years in school in exchange for some clear economic benefit. Instead, they are expected, or even conditioned, to work in exchange for some anticipated economic benefit that may or may not come their way. Education is compulsory in much of the world and even if individuals generally benefit from a strong economy, they most certainly don't benefit equally. Many scarcely benefit at all.[9] Nor is there adequate evidence to support the claim that an education geared toward career and college preparation best promotes economic growth. The correlation between economic prosperity and education is not clear-cut and it is possible that the economic benefits of schooling are just as well or even better served by schools that feature a broader educational mission than one geared primarily toward the economy.

---

[9] Alexander Sidorkin argues that the true beneficiaries of this system are the businesses that rely on school-trained, low-paid employees, our society that depends on a combination of low- and high-skill workers, and the third of students who use schooling as a stepping stone to attend and complete their university studies. The remaining two-thirds of students who do not attain a university degree can expect to receive average salaries hovering close to the poverty line for a family of four, see Alexander Sidorkin, "Is Schooling a Consumer Good? A Case against School Choice But Not the One You Had in Mind," *Philosophy of Education 2007*, ed. Nicholas Burbules (Urbana: Philosophy of Education Society, 2007).

Despite the undeniable influence of this way of thinking about education, most schools do not strictly adhere to such a narrow purpose. The economic justification for public education represents only one motivation for administrators and teachers alike. In fact, it is unclear whether even the strongest proponents of this approach consistently hold such dogmatic views. An examination of the mission statements of high schools attended by children of the political and economic elite underscores this point. It is here, in these mission statements, rather than in policies and mission statements of schools meant for other children, that one can glimpse more ambitious aims for education. Take, for example, the school that the daughter of former governor Snyder attended:

> OUR MISSION—Greenhills School is a student-centered community that helps young people realize their full intellectual, ethical, artistic and athletic potential in preparation for college—and beyond—as curious, creative, and responsible citizens who respect all individuals and their differences, and whose meaningful and balanced lives will better the world.
>
> Greenhills School[10]

Or the mission statements of other elite schools throughout the world:

> VISION—educating the whole child, Eton School inspires creative, confident thinkers who have an enduring passion for learning and are poised to contribute to the world.
>
> A LIVING MISSION STATEMENT—At most schools, the mission statement is a set document from year to year. At Eton School, the mission statement is a living document reviewed, discussed, revised (if needed) and signed by the teachers and administrators each year during our August inservice. We do this because we not only believe in our mission, we live it!

---

[10] "What Makes Greenhills Exceptional," *Greenhills School*. Accessed April 7, 2019. https://www.greenhillsschool.org/about/our-purpose/.

We at Eton School commit to educate the whole child and honor the diversity of each individual, intellectually, emotionally, socially, physically, and spiritually. We support this Mission by providing developmentally designed programs and methodologies based on Montessori philosophy and educational research. We dedicate ourselves to lifelong learning.

Eton School, UK[11]

OUR PURPOSE is to inspire our students and community to flourish and make a positive difference through our unique and transformational education adventures

OUR FOCUS is learning to flourish

OUR SPIRIT is making a positive difference

OUR CHARACTER is to be authentic, courageous, dedicated, forgiving, inquiring, loving, optimistic, passionate, resilient and trusting

WE BELIEVE our rigorous academic programmes create wonder, curiosity and a desire to learn . . . Positive Education enhances wellbeing and enables individuals to flourish . . .

OUR CHALLENGE is to develop creative thinking and learning to engage with the complex opportunities of a changing world.

Geelong Grammar School, Australia[12]

MISSION—Upper Canada College provides transformational learning experiences that foster the development of head, heart and humanity, and inspire each boy to make a lasting and positive impact on his world.

Upper Canada College, Toronto Canada[13]

Exeter today continues the commitment to unite knowledge and goodness. It seeks students who combine proven academic ability,

---

[11] "Vision and Mission," *Eton School*. Accessed April 7, 2019. https://www.etonschool.org/about/visionmission.

[12] "Our Purpose," *Geelong Grammar School*. Accessed April 7, 2019. https://www.ggs.vic.edu.au/School/Our-School/our-purpose.

[13] "Vision and Mission," *Upper Canada College*. Accessed April 7, 2019. https://www.ucc.on.ca/welcome/vision-and-mission.

intellectual curiosity, and tenacity with decency and good character. At the Academy, exacting inquiry and thoughtful discourse foster the life of the mind, instruction and activity promote fitness and health, and the daily interactions of a residential school nurture integrity, empathy, and kindness. Because learning and growth at Exeter arise from each individual's engagement with others, the richness of education here requires diversity in all its dimensions; students and faculty value the differences they bring to the community they share.

Phillips Exeter Academy, US[14]

Setting aside all questions concerning whether such schools actually achieve these lofty aims, or whether the main draw of these schools has more to do with the social and economic advantages of attending them, these mission statements reinforce the intuition that what constitutes an education is something significantly more than high test scores and future economic success. At these and other elite schools, teachers are charged with the task of helping children lead active, flourishing lives beyond the economic realm (reflecting of course the confidence that economic benefits will flow the way of their students nonetheless). The mission statements and core liberal arts curriculum of many colleges and universities reflect this broader vision as well.

Before addressing what this vision involves, consider a response from the standpoint of critical theory. Making the comparison between the rhetoric of human capital proponents and the kind of education they want for their own children leads many very reasonably to conclude that the purpose of education varies according to a child's class and status in society. Familiarity with the history of schooling reinforces this suspicion as tracking students by class, ethnicity and gender, rather than by academic talent alone, is a common practice in most Western democracies. Critical theorists make a stronger claim. They argue that the underlying function of schools is to reproduce class and other

---

[14] "Academy Mission Statement," *Phillips Exeter Academy*. Accessed April 7, 2019. http://64.140.204.145/about_us/171_9259.aspx.

divisions. Mission statements, as ideological documents in education, they insist, mask a more insidious purpose, which is to keep students in their place.[15]

In counterpoint, critical theorists press their own societal designs on education. Rather than perpetuate the current economic system which they claim benefits only the few, schools should function to actively bring about a more just society.[16] Although theorists in this tradition differ in their approaches to or even conceptions of justice, all are united in challenging the human capital paradigm and its perpetuation of the status quo which they see as not only inherently classist but also racist, sexist, and homophobic. In contrast to the core idea implicit in the dominant paradigm—that everyone has a role to play in contributing to and benefiting from the fruits of a well-functioning society—many critical theorists turn to conflict theory for an explanatory model. In an unequal society, what benefits the dominant group tends to harm subordinate groups. That is, there is an inescapable conflict between the class interests of those located on the different socioeconomic levels of a deeply unequal, stratified society. Given this outlook, the purpose espoused by many critical theorists is one of revolutionary *praxis* which calls on teachers to wake students from their complacent slumber and not only identify but also work to rectify injustices in society. Reverting to their own form of utilitarian calculation, critical theorists see education as a valuable vehicle for effecting broad sociopolitical change and realizing their vision of a more just society.

A rigid adherence to this political mission makes critical theory vulnerable to some of the same objections leveled against the

---

[15] For two influential versions of this argument, see Pierre Bourdieu and Jean-Claude Passeron, *Reproduction in Education, Society and Culture*, 2nd edn. (London: Sage Press, 2000) and Samuel Bowles and Herbert Gintis, *Schooling in Capitalist America: Educational Reform and the Contradictions of Economic Life* (Chicago: Haymarket Books, 2011).

[16] For three examples of critical theory, see Paulo Freire, *Pedagogy of the Oppressed: 30th Anniversary Edition* (New York: Bloomsbury Academic, 2014); bell hooks, *Teaching to Transgress: Education as the Practice of Freedom* (New York: Routledge, 1994); Michael Apple, *Ideology and Curriculum*, 4th edn. (New York: Routledge, 2019).

human capital paradigm. There is an inevitable tension within the field concerning the appropriate relationship between educational and political ends. Some might accuse critical theorists of treating students as pawns of a political movement rather than individuals with their own interests and ideas about the world.[17] At the same time, critical theory's strong liberatory and pluralistic commitments, along with its utopian origins, might mitigate this tendency. If applied correctly, critical theorists argue, their activist approach to teaching will emancipate individual students from the weight of the dominant culture, while also providing them with the tools and a voice to effect broad political change. Teachers, on this view, face a choice between advancing the interests of the dominant society, or working on behalf of the freedom and dignity of students trapped in the status quo of an unjust social order.[18]

Of course, the human capital and critical theory paradigms compete with other social-political visions of education. Religious leaders, progressive educators, techno-enthusiasts, environmentalists, and many other concerned citizens call on public education to remedy various social ills, preserve cherished traditions, and prepare students to address the many demands of society. Supporters of each of these groups vie for public support and a seat at the school reform table. In fact, debates such as these have been waged since the advent of public education. If Robert Hitchens was right to conclude

---

[17] Early critical theorists, like members of the Frankfurt School, were pessimistic about our ability to simply fix social problems using calculative, instrumental reason. See for instance, Max Horkeimer, *The Eclipse of Reason* (New York: Bloomsbury Academic, 2013). Some more recent critical theorists, such as Paulo Freire, have criticized political activists who foist their own formulas and principles top-down without listening to the people. At the same time, it is unclear whether Freire's own work suffers from similar problems as dialogue moves to collective action. In the search for political results, there is the temptation to separate those who resist the Truth (and thus suffer from false consciousness and the internalization of an oppressor ideology) from those who possess the right insights into their oppression in a way that spurs revolutionary action. Freire, *Pedagogy of the Oppressed*.

[18] William Ayers, *Teaching Toward Freedom: Moral Commitment and Ethical Action in the Classroom* (Boston: Beacon Press, 2005).

that "the character of education is determined by the character of society," then it is not surprising that broad sociopolitical aims have a prominent place in our conception of the purpose of and justification for public education.[19]

These aims and justifications, however, do not exhaust education's purpose, nor can they ultimately dictate the full range of pedagogical intent that teachers express in their work. The mission statements presented above reaffirm the clear sense that education is not confined to broad societal purposes. Questioning whether these mission statements mask reality or articulate entrenched privilege is certainly appropriate, but such questions say little about the value of the aims themselves. Nor do valid objections to entrenched privilege deny that such aims often find their way, often thanks to dedicated teachers, into underprivileged schools. What these mission statements do reveal is an ambitious vision of education that starts with the flourishing of the individual as the basis of a flourishing society. If we want a fuller appreciation of purpose in teaching, it is perhaps here—in the flourishing of individual students— that we should look.

Purpose and Student Flourishing

Ms. Zelenski doesn't teach abstract wage earners or nondescript members of some oppressed group; she teaches Denzel, Anika, Malia, Philip, and Raymond—all unique individuals, all passionate about something, and all personally affected to varying degrees by inequality and the violence, drugs, and poverty, as well as the joys, achievements, and close bonds of their neighborhood. Whatever the venue, subject, or sociopolitical context, teachers must teach individuals who come with their own unique hopes, insecurities, intentions, and talents.

---

[19] Robert M. Hutchins, "Ideals in Education," *The American Journal of Sociology* 43, no. 1 (1937): 1.

This fact is not lost on most teachers. Given the relational nature of teaching, it would be hard to ignore. It is therefore not surprising that there is often a wide gap between institutional aims and the intentions of teachers, students, and even parents.[20] While politicians and theorists might concentrate on broad economic and political trends, such considerations make up only a small portion of the daily motivations of teachers. Not only are teachers more attuned to completing short-term goals—for example, getting a concept across properly or completing an activity—but their teaching is also imbued with a broader sense of purpose, such as Zelenski's attempt to instill a love of reading. On the ground, teachers have their own agenda and visions of what constitutes success.

Michael Oakeshott defends a conception of education that is fundamentally at odds with the modern view that education should serve some extrinsic social purpose. For him, we acquire purpose from the activities we engage in and not the other way around. "Human beings," he writes, "do not start from rest and spring into activity only when attracted by a purpose to be achieved. To be alive is to be perpetually active. The purposes we attribute to particular kinds of activity are only abridgments of our knowledge of how to engage in this or that activity."[21] In other words, purpose emerges through our engagement within various, ongoing kinds of activity. For Oakeshott, the true value of education lies in our ability to free ourselves from our immediate physical environment and recognize ourselves in a larger sphere of meaning. One's quality of life, in other words, results from one's world of "understanding, imagining, meanings, moral and religious beliefs, relationships, practices—states of mind in which the human condition is to be discerned as recognition of and responses to the ordeal of

---

[20] Danielle Allen goes so far as to say that institutional justifications of education are logically distinct from "justifications of particular instances of teaching," just as the explanation of baseball is leisure but the actual practice of baseball is tied to scoring more runs, and so on. Allen, *Education and Equality*, 10–11.

[21] Michael Oakeshott, *The Voice of Liberal Learning* (Indianapolis: Liberty Fund, 2001), 104.

consciousness."[22] We therefore make a fatal mistake when we replace education with socialization, or reduce it to "an apprenticeship to adult life—teaching, training, instructing, imparting knowledge, learning, etc.—governed by an extrinsic purpose."[23] While education is certainly not socially valueless, Oakeshott believes it is corrupted when extrinsic rewards become, by design, its end.

This is a startling claim to many contemporary ears, and yet Oakeshott represents a rich and long tradition that associates education with the active life of the mind. While few are as dogmatic in their rejection of education's external benefits, the humanist ideals and sensibilities he defends are still present in many conceptions of education today. "Education," writes Oakeshott, "is not acquiring a stock of ready-made ideas, images, sentiments, beliefs and so forth; it is learning to look, to listen, to think, to feel, to imagine, to believe, to understand, to choose and to wish."[24] There are surely teachers for whom this is purpose enough to carry forward in their work.

Danielle Allen espouses a version of these ideals but does not see the external and internal values of education as fundamentally incompatible. She believes that institutional (macro-level) justifications for education, which always take some form of utilitarian calculation, can work side by side with micro-level justifications that are more focused on awakening the latent human potentials of individual students. Allen believes that this latter perspective, what she calls *eudaimonistic* (after the Greek word for flourishing), is the perspective that most teachers take while engaged in the throes of teaching.[25] That is, teachers naturally attend to the development of their students *as individuals* and cultivate in them understandings, virtues and values that are, in effect, ends in themselves. In Zelenski's English class, what matters are those times

---

[22] Oakeshott, *The Voice of Liberal Learning*, 100 and 103.

[23] Oakeshott, *The Voice of Liberal Learning*, 91.

[24] Oakeshott, *The Voice of Liberal Learning*, 67.

[25] Allen, *Education and Equality*, 11.

when, for example, Denzel has just devoured his novel, Malia shows signs of having really grown up in the last few weeks, and Raymond and Philip no longer complain about reading in silence. Here, reading literature is good regardless of whether doing so will help her students secure a job, impress friends, or develop better communication skills. No doubt, these benefits are admirable and partly justify why we have public education in the first place, but they are not the whole story.

While there is no fundamental incompatibility between the human capital approach and the *eudaimonistic* approach, Allen does worry about the possibility that institutional concerns will obscure, even replace, the *eudaimonistic* mission of teachers. When teachers are overburdened by learning objectives guided by narrow state interests, there is little time to expose students to the many other facets of education. Education is therefore impoverished when it is reduced to some instrumental value.

Drawing from Hannah Arendt's democratic theory, Allen provides a "humanistic baseline" of human potentials that combine institutional and *eudaimonistic* interests, and includes something essential for critical theorists as well. She calls for an education oriented to the development of four broad capacities, namely:

1. Prepare ourselves for breadwinning work
2. Prepare ourselves for civic and political engagement
3. Prepare ourselves for creative self-expression and world-making (in the Arendtian sense, see Chapter 2)
4. Prepare ourselves for rewarding relationships in spaces of intimacy and leisure.

She continues:

> We recognize that the capacities relevant to all these domains are flourishing when we see young people become adults who can support themselves economically without exploiting others, take their place among a world of adult creators, including as creators of rewarding intimate relationships, and participate effectively in their polity's political life. When the humanistic baseline for the micro-level concept

of education is given content from such democratic *eudaimonism*, it orients us toward a pedagogic practice that is in itself egalitarian in that it seeks to meet the same range of needs for all students.[26]

Allen's conception of education may be too pragmatic for Oakeshott, but it is perhaps appropriate for a democratic society as envisioned by Arendt that seeks to activate a "potential that inheres in all human beings—as a feature of the human condition—to succeed at labor, work and political action simultaneously."[27] Not surprisingly, we find similar commitments in the mission statements mentioned earlier in this chapter.

The advocates of both human capital theory and critical theory may conceivably incorporate their own visions of individual flourishing within the landscape of these ideas. For those thinking in terms of human capital, Allen's emphasis on personal autonomy and the free pursuit of meaningful work and economic success is appealing. Meanwhile, from the perspective of critical theory, the vision of a diverse and egalitarian society where a *eudaimonistic* spirit can thrive in us all is fundamental. bell hooks captures this sense of flourishing when she writes:

> To educate as the practice of freedom is a way of teaching that anyone can learn. That learning process comes easiest to those of us who teach who also believe that there is an aspect of our vocation that is sacred: who believe that our word is not merely to share information but to share in the intellectual and spiritual growth of our students. To teach in a manner that respects and cares for the souls of our students is essential if we are to provide the necessary conditions where learning can most deeply and intimately begin.[28]

There are many other ways in which societal and individual aims might converge to form a coherent vision of education. Since the nineteenth century, the German notion of *Bildung* (a term with no suitable

---

[26] Allen, *Education and Equality*, 17.

[27] Allen, *Education and Equality*, 16.

[28] hooks, *Teaching to Transgress*, 13.

English equivalent) has represented a view of education in which the cultivation of the humanity and rationality of individuals forms the basis of political ideals governing participation in civil society. In this conception, the flourishing of the state is intimately connected to the flourishing of individuals.[29] In many liberal societies, this notion takes on a more individualist bent—the idea that, in the interest of student flourishing, teachers should place greater emphasis upon their capacity for autonomy and self-sufficiency, over and above the parental and cultural values and norms that predominate where they happen to live.[30] Tensions invariably exist in the ways that the relationship between individual and community are understood in the context of teaching, reminding teachers of the need to consider their purposes in such matters.

Perhaps, in the end, the temptation to specify the *true* purpose of education is misguided. If we examine the full diversity of educational settings and subjects, we might reach the conclusion that a better question to ask is how a teacher's purposefulness is connected to her own cares and the cares of her students. We might find that pleasurable, aesthetic, or rather mundane cares override political, economic, and moral ones. Oakeshott may be right that the articulation of mission statements and other educational purposes puts the cart before the horse. Purposes emerge from the worlds we inhabit. What we understand provides purpose, and not the other way around. According to this logic, purpose might gradually evolve in the teaching process as a teacher comes to understand her students or subject matter differently or she decides, for no particular reason, to shift attention to something new and unanticipated. In fact, teachers can get along quite well—better than perhaps many might like to admit—without any overarching purpose. At this point, teaching might become a chore,

---

[29] For an analysis of this perspective, see Gert Biesta, "How General Can *Bildung* Be? Reflections on a Future of a Modern Educational Ideal," *Journal of Philosophy of Education* 36, no. 3 (2002).

[30] For one such example, see Brighouse, *On Education*.

but maybe not. Perhaps teaching has no other purpose than doing what a teacher sets out to do. Nevertheless, it is the *enduring pedagogical intent* that distinguishes teaching from learning or instruction in other contexts. These intentions may be carefully considered or misbegotten and short-sighted, but purpose emerges one way or the other.

Problems of Purpose

There are few things in life more reassuring than a deeply settled sense of purpose. At times, teachers enjoy such clarity. An acknowledged master teaching a dedicated apprentice might never have cause to question the purpose, nor would the one grateful for the opportunity to be taught. There are no doubt many cases that are less extreme but similar in being quite straightforward as to the articulated purposes being served. But in most instances of teaching, purpose is more problematic, something subject to conflicting interests, ambiguity, and doubt. Teachers often work at cross-purposes and the connection between short-term goals and general aims is often tenuous at best.

In Denby's account, Ms. Zelenski questions the state-mandated curriculum, her students' interests, and even the value of her own efforts to expose her students to reading. While it is clear that she acts purposefully, her purposes and intentions are difficult to state precisely and can fade quickly as she steps back and reflects on her work. This is true for many teachers. And not only teachers; parents, politicians, administrators, and the general public also worry about the various, intersecting, sometimes conflicting goals and aims of teaching. Whenever and from whatever perspective they are articulated, it seems that everyone has a stake in a teacher's purposes. The work of teachers can be seen as a means to fix our problems, preserve our values, and identify the best futures for our children. It can also lead to dismay when education isn't up to the task. A lack of consensus about what education is and should be only deepens our anxieties further, and creates a sense of urgency to get a handle on the purposes that ought to be served in teaching.

To whom does that work fall? As we noted in the previous section, in many ways, the sense of purpose emerges within the work of teaching; general aims and broad purposes, on that view, provide a kind of orientation, within which the more specific, ever-changing, intersubjective experience of teachers and students becomes purposeful over time—as with Ms. Zelinski. Many teachers see that as the nature of the work; the anxieties and uncertainties of purpose are often just part of the process.

Others, however, respond to such anxieties by advancing efforts designed to enforce clearly defined purposes to be served, minimizing the discretion of teachers to adjust their intentions and purposes in the bargain. In earlier chapters, we addressed the common ways in which systems of managerial control distort teaching. This is especially the case when we abbreviate considerations of purpose by focusing upon purposes tied to fixed, quantifiable indicators, such as test scores or graduation rates. But this strategy is unlikely to produce good results. A notable finding of social science, "Campbell's Law," states that "the more any quantitative social indicator is used for social decision-making, the more subject it will be to corruption pressures and the more apt it will be to distort and corrupt the social processes it is intended to monitor."[31] Both the indicator and the process being governed are vulnerable to corrupting kinds of distortion. This is especially evident in the common practice of translating general aims and purposes into measurable outcomes. Consider Ms. Zielinski once again. If the sole indicator of her success is taken to be some specific measure of reading comprehension, how reliable will the test be over time? And how might the emphasis on such a measure distort her wider vision of what it means to encourage a love of reading in her students? If her wider

---

[31] Quoted in Daniel Koretz, *Measuring Up: What Educational Testing Really Tell Us?* (Cambridge: Harvard University Press, 2009), 237.

vision of reading is indeed a richly purposeful one, then the distorting effects of the imposed measure, by placing emphasis on attaining good test scores, would undermine her sense of purpose.

Finally, where issues about purpose in teaching are concerned, technological innovation is a significant factor and may bring about a sea change in thinking about the way purpose is understood in practice. A profusion of ventures now advance forms of digitized and online instruction as an inexpensive and efficacious response to the problem of purpose. The underlying logic of online offerings involves the creation of content that captures the attention and satisfies the interests of those who partake of it. Where educational offerings are concerned, this way of thinking converts students into consumers choosing among the expanding range of programs, courses, and other offerings generated by curriculum designers and providers. What will the role of teachers be in such transactions? In many cases, they will be actively engaged in the design of what is offered, as well as in managing student learning in online programs and courses. But the scope of cares they can express and attend to, the range of aims, explicit and implicit, that they can pursue, potentially will be very different in ways that remain to be seen.

Where managerial and technological initiatives lead and how they ultimately impact the role of teachers in the formation and understanding of purpose in education are matters of profound interest. They represent challenges to the latitude teachers traditionally have had in practice where the articulation of purpose is concerned. Whether teachers have been given too much latitude in the past is a matter of debate, but neither managerial controls nor online systems resolve the inherent issues that surround how purpose is conceived in practice.

Why Purpose Matters

In this chapter we have addressed the way notions of purpose are infused in teaching, and the range of ways to think about and justify what is taking place. The sense of purpose is in some ways the public face of care in teaching, and as with care, getting clear about purpose is complicated. But whereas care originates as a motivational feature of a teacher's work, purpose often originates in broad social and political contexts of meaning. We submitted Danielle Allen's humanistic baseline as a possible blueprint for combining macro-level and micro-level concerns to guide public education. But such broad blueprints leave a great deal to work out in the actual, distinct situations of practice.

How ideas of purpose are worked out in practice is a revealing and pivotal component of education. A clear sense of purpose is a powerful thing, but as teachers know, there are contending sources of purpose to sort out and make sense of in their work with students. A heightened capacity to proceed purposefully is surely one of the finest things a teacher can bestow on those with whom they work, though questions will always remain about the purposes that prevail.

Thinking about your own experience teaching and being taught

- Considering the range of purposes teachers have articulated in your experience, what purposes have been most influential in your life and which ones failed to impress?
- How important is the sense of purpose in the quality of educational experiences and what is the teacher's role in that regard?

Thinking about conceptions and theories of purpose in teaching

- Which of the purposes described in this chapter do you find most compelling? Why?
- How well does Danielle Allen's attempt to draw together societal goals and individual flourishing work in your view?

Thinking about how purpose relates to the other elements of teaching

- How do purposes imposed from above influence the way teachers express and act upon what they care about? Conversely, how do the cares of teachers influence purpose in the classroom?
- What and whose purposes are most important to satisfy where subject matter is concerned?

Thinking about purpose in other contexts of life

- What have teachers helped you to understand, intentionally or not, about the sources, questions, and meaning of purpose and purposefulness in life?
- In what ways have your teachers fallen short or even led you astray in this regard?

7

Establishing a Sense of Place

It is 7:30 on a Monday morning and McKenzie, age 12, wakes up, kisses her Chihuahua, Ringo, says good morning to her parents, and gets ready to jet off to her classes at an academy that specializes in teaching math, science and engineering. She attends school on Mondays and Wednesdays, taking classes in pre-algebra, history and English with 15 other students. Her teachers stay in contact with her, as well as with her parents, by e-mail and a program called SnapGrades . . .

Thursdays are different for McKenzie. She catches up on work for her classes, works on her weekly history essay with guidance from her tutor via e-mail (and from her dad from his classroom 20 miles away and from her mom who works in a home office), and works on her grammar skills in a self-paced course at Universal-Class.com. Next, McKenzie uses an online math program to help her grasp challenging concepts, reads a chapter in her history book, then meets with her French tutor at a local coffee shop. The meeting is conducted entirely in French since McKenzie hopes to become fluent and one day live in France.

On the same Monday morning McKenzie's 15-year-old sister, Madison, takes her terrier for a walk while she listens to a lecture on psychology from a Pulitzer Prize-winning professor and then a lecture on history from a Stanford University professor, both downloaded from iTunes U to her iPod. Once back at her desk, she puts in a DVD and watches a lecture on geometry for a course. Next she uses her computer to "attend" a class from a self-paced online MIT biology course, then meets with her supervising teacher to review her progress in preparation for the high school exit exam. Later in the day, her language arts tutor, and associate professor at Stanford University who works for the gifted and talented program, meets her at the local park where they discuss Pride and Prejudice.

> *On Tuesdays and Thursdays, Madison, who has a passion for Jane Austen, physically attends a course on British literature at Sacramento State University. . . . On her way home, Madison stops at a special event on campus and she signs up for a workshop for aspiring authors, where she'll share the novel she is writing. Later in the day, Madison completes a Chinese language lesson online and e-mails her completed essay to her tutor for final editing.*
>
> Elizabeth Kanna, Lisa Gillis, and Christina Culver, *Virtual Schooling*[1]

McKenzie and Madison are presented as harbingers of a new world of education. They work with and benefit from teachers and one imagines that the elements of teaching we have addressed to this point still apply in the teaching they access. What is being celebrated in this case (drawn from a book about "optimizing" education) is the sense of freedom McKenzie and Madison enjoy. In particular, their freedom is derived from shifting the locus of control over how and where their time is spent. "Virtual schooling" means that they, unlike their peers in school, are not stuck in a place not of their own choosing. They both do spend time in the company of teachers—both online and face-to-face—but it is clear that what matters is how well that time contributes to their personal goals. Places of learning, whether online or actual, either serve their interests or, presumably, are a waste of time.

This is a striking departure where teaching is concerned. The activities of teaching have traditionally been situated in particular settings of some kind. Not only is the place of teaching designed for and defined by the particular pedagogical purposes being served, say a kindergarten or chemistry lab, but the place of teaching is also meaningful in providing the ground for teachers and students to gather together as all the elements of teaching unfold over time. The *sense of place* in teaching is richly composed of diverse cares and purposes, the dynamics of authority in practice, the situational demands of virtue and practical judgment, and the complex features of the subject matter. Such

---

[1] Elizabeth Kanna, Lisa Gills, and Christina Culver, *Virtual Schooling: A Guide to Optimizing Your Child's Education* (New York: St. Martin's Press, 2009), 7–8.

things do not happen in a vacuum or on demand; teaching transpires in an inherently meaningful, though distinctly malleable place.

Efforts to establish a sense of place are of course complex, involving as they do not only particular teachers and their students but also interested parties, including educational administrators, with a stake in how the place of teaching is to be structured and utilized. Teachers, for their part, do the best they can with what they have. Because all teaching is situated in a meaningful context, teachers are right to dwell as they do on how best to shape the setting so as to make the most of it.

What does it mean to make the most of it, however? Those celebrating the freedom of McKenzie and Madison have a point. The place of teaching is as ambiguous as teaching itself. Some places stimulate and liberate the mind while others inhibit and confine; places of teaching can be designed to encourage all sorts of approaches and orientations to learning. Thinking about how teachers work to establish the sense of place in teaching is therefore a matter of genuine concern to all involved.

In this chapter, we take up this concern. First, we consider ways in which teachers address the spatial and temporal parameters of their work—the basic constraints of place. The constraints of place may be deeply rewarding, though they are often experienced as a burden. This is where the promise of technologically mediated instruction registers. We explore why this is so, but wonder what is lost when one turns toward the "virtual places" of online learning. We conclude by suggesting the value of rethinking place in teaching. Our contention is that, for teachers, the quality of relationships and learning they seek to foster is bound up in considerations of the kind of place they manage to create.

The Constraints of Place in Teaching

All teachers must navigate the spatial and temporal constraints that situate their teaching in a particular here and now. Throughout millennia, teachers of all sorts have managed to do this in a variety of likely and unlikely settings. Whatever the setting, the task set before teachers is to bring about the conditions for the activities of teaching to unfold in a desirable way. What is regarded as desirable varies enormously of course. But what is common to all teaching is the need to take account of the basic constraints of time and space one has to work within and to make of them a place for one's teaching to transpire.

Let's take a closer look at how the sense of place comes about and what it involves. Place, according to Yi-Fu Tuan, is distinct from space. While space is the abstract and largely nondescript gap between point A and point B, place is pregnant with the significance of experience and tradition. "What begins as undifferentiated space," writes Tuan, "becomes place as we get to know it better and endow it with value."[2] Place occasions a fuller experience. While space is largely a product of our vision, both literally and figuratively, most people experience place with all five senses. A carpenter's apprentice, for example, experiences a workshop invested with the smells of freshly cut wood, and of lacquers and glues; the sounds of concentrated activity; the sights and feel of cold tools, soft rags; and the distinctive colors of oak, pine, and maple.

While one is invited to manipulate space, place manipulates you. Apprentices enter the shop and soak up the energy of the place. If things come together as they should, the workshop will evoke in them respect for the authority of the master carpenter and professional pride in the tasks undertaken. Classroom spaces, though in most cases much less stimulating to the senses, are nonetheless staged with a similar intent. Amphitheater seating suits the lecture hall, but a circle of desks, or better yet a table, promotes discussion. A well-staged classroom will direct proper attention and care to what is being taught, augment the authority of the teacher, and contextualize roles and expectations. Even someone who is normally quiet and unassuming can become transformed as she assumes the position of teacher with "the right staging and props, the right time and place."

---

[2] Yi-Fu Tuan, *Space and Place* (Minneapolis: University of Minnesota Press, 1977), 6.

At the center of an individual's sense of place is the body. The physical presence of teachers and students together has a profound impact on educational experience. Contemporary critics of face-to-face teaching sometimes overlook this feature. Others lament the fact that the physical arrangement of bodies in traditional schools has not dramatically changed in the last century. Students are often put in their place according to age, subject, and talent; many students still spend most of their time sitting in rows of desks facing the instructor. Nevertheless, attempts to replace these arrangements with something else, for example, multiaged classrooms, integrated subjects, and open concept classrooms is testament to the importance of the embodied presence of students and the way in which the landscape marks students as they find their place within it.

Unlike education in its virtual contexts, the embodied presence of participants demands a certain sensitivity and responsiveness from the teacher. A subtle shift in the mood of the audience or the mere look of incredulity on the face of students may warrant a change of pace or the looping back to an earlier point.[3] The teacher draws from a stock of body language, tones of voice, turns of phrases, and gestural habits to convey her message. She reads the messages students provide in the same ways. Irony, for instance, is most effective when students can discern a difference between the words spoken and the tone and facial expression of the teacher. Sometimes a mere look speaks volumes. Paul Woodruff's point that an "unforgettable silence" may be the only way to bring attention to the enormity of the subject matter is only one of many uses of silence routinely utilized by experienced teachers.[4] As a speech act, of course, silence requires an audience to witness the one

---

[3]   In this section, we draw from our earlier work, Paul Farber and Dini Metro-Roland, "Being on One's Way: Place, Technology and the Moral Commodification of Education," *Philosophy of Education 2013*, ed. Cris Mayo (Urbana, IL: Philosophy of Education Society, 2014).

[4]   Paul Woodruff, *Reverence: Renewing a Forgotten Virtue* (New York: Oxford University Press, 2001), 188.

who chooses not to speak (something that is not easily done on most online learning platforms).

Such sensitivity and responsiveness are not reserved for the teachers alone. An integral part of the educative process for students is acquiring the ability to read the physical gestures and expressions, moods and emotions of others, while developing one's own communicative cues and strategies. While there are certainly rules of engagement—raise your hand, don't interrupt others— the majority of situations call for deeper recognition without the benefits of formulas. Experienced participants of classroom culture learn to react to social situations without internal deliberation— they instinctively know what's asked of them from taking in their surroundings. This is what Herbert Dreyfus means when he argues that the complex dynamics of situated learning triggers in the learner a capacity to take risks, a readiness for surprise, and a commitment to meaningful learning that enables competent learners to make the qualitative leap beyond mere rule-following to embrace greater complexity, as well as new challenges and demands.[5] As our chapter on the cultivation of virtue suggests, it often takes time for students to get to the point where they feel enough at home to become contributing members of the classroom. Extensive time in a place, that is, in a particular social group assembled to grapple with particular subject matter, is a necessary part of this educative process.

What students learn to do extends beyond the official curriculum. Like all places, classrooms inscribe values that both reinforce and challenge norms and traditions. We learn how to watch and be watched, speak and listen, move and remain still in specific ways. We develop a sense of self by mimicking others and reacting to the categories in which we are placed. In schools and elsewhere, we are also called to trade places with strangers especially when their realities clash with our

---

[5]   Hubert Dreyfus, *On the Internet* (New York: Routledge, 2001), 72–88.

prejudgments and past experiences. These interactions are dialogical in nature; as we understand one another more deeply, we also come to better understand ourselves.

Being physically present with others in a classroom thus sets it apart from learning in isolation or in anonymity. This is true not only because the context permits dynamic relationships between individuals but also because the students develop a stronger sense of a community of learners. As John Dewey reminds us, such places supply "one of the most important lessons of life, that of mutual accommodation and adaptation."[6]

Of course, such accommodations function in myriad ways. What constitutes the proper conventions of educational engagement is fluid and varies according to subject matter, venue and the actions, moods, and cultural background of participants.[7] But even in the cases where there appears to be a lack of genuine respect, goodwill, or group solidarity the effect of a shared place can create the conditions for these feelings to emerge. Of course, there is risk here as well. Critical theorists are right to remind us that bodies and identities are often shaped by powerful social norms that reinforce inequalities of class, ethnicity, gender, sexuality, and ability. Trading places with others, submitting to the conventions of a group, and finding one's place in a group are clearly more perilous for some than others.

Where the experience of place is concerned, the particular contribution of time constraints must be noted as well. Time constraints seem to be a ubiquitous feature of teaching, affecting both, for teachers, the planning, application, and evaluation of teaching and, for students, their sense of commitment—for better or worse— to being physically present for a predetermined duration of time. Whether one is excited to be in some place, or woeful about being

---

[6]   Dewey, *Experience and Education*, 60.

[7]   For a more detailed treatment of this, see Farber and Metro-Roland, "The Promise and Limits of Online Learning."

stuck there, the sense of time and the way it passes is on everyone's mind. If time were not an issue, teaching—like all other human activities—would be radically different.

It is tempting to set aside the qualitative characteristics of time and focus on a more reliable and objective division of time into distinct, equal units of calculation. In fact, the instrumental view of teaching strongly encourages such an orientation. It is easier to organize and manage teaching if we view it as a linear progression of segments, lessons, units, semesters, years, and so on. A similar calculus is implicit in developmental theories, scheduling, grade designations, benchmarks, credentialing, and in the very logic of our outcome-obsessed culture. Just about everything a teacher does can be broken down into intervals of time that can be subsequently subjected to independent analysis and cross-comparison. If a minute, hour or day is uniform everywhere, then we have a standard basis of measurement from which to evaluate teaching across settings. Such calculations also furnish teachers with a way to check their own performance against past work, guiding them toward the continual pursuit of more efficient and effective practices yielding the results that they want.

The narrative arc of teaching, however, is no straight and narrow path. While many of the temporal features of teaching are broken down in measurable units, time marks teaching in more subtle ways as well. Perhaps it suffices to remind the reader of the ways in which an hour can fly by or drag on forever. Students and teachers experience the present through a rich and tangled past and can only reflect back on what they learn through the *camera obscura* of memory. How these memories are organized and interpreted is not incidental to the educational process. They form the very heart of what it is to be educated. What is retained and the manner in which it is retained and valued is often intimately connected to the context in which it is encountered. That school is a place set apart from all others impinges on the quality and meaning of these memories. Consider how often we understand our past and construct our identities around culturally infused periods of educational experience: the places we detested, those we found tolerable, and those where good fortune reigned and we found ourselves for a time in what seemed to be exactly the right place.

Liberating Learning?

Isn't that precisely what McKenzie and Madison are looking for, some optimal sequence of benefits resulting from being in the right place at the right time? Madison and MacKenzie stand in for an idea, namely, that it is now possible for the first time to conceive of limitless kinds of learning freed from the constraints of traditional settings established and maintained by teachers.

Make no mistake, this has the makings of a revolution. While it isn't difficult to point out glaring failures in the array of initiatives thus far advanced, it is easy for proponents of emerging technologies to point to new technological fixes in the works. Whatever you might worry about in Madison and MacKenzie's setting, it has probably been altered already and possibly surpassed. New possibilities are always on the way. That this vignette may already feel outdated is testament to the rapidity of technological innovation.

The promise of new technologies for learning is that learners will be liberated from the settings managed by teachers that have traditionally restricted students' movement and dictated the place and time, the pace, tone, and content of learning throughout the formative years of most people's lives. Their hope is that we can separate the confining aspects of teaching from the satisfying and meaningful parts. Proponents do this by maximizing utility in terms of both the design of instructional platforms and materials and the heightened sense of learner agency. If designers and learners can identify what is and will be useful, then we can streamline learning without the costly and cumbersome features of the classroom or the inefficient idiosyncrasies of the teacher. Why worry about teaching all kinds of things that may be useful in some distant future when we can now focus on learning what we need *when* we need it. This mindset of focusing on what's "useful" reinforces the tendency, we noted elsewhere, to think about why teaching matters in terms of its immediate instrumental value, what and whom it is good for, and how best to maximize the outcomes that are desired.[8]

Since the rise of compulsory education in the modern era, schooling has featured a long-standing preoccupation with efficiency and scientific management that puts the onus on time management and a uniformity of instruction. Control is a product of time management and the ability of the teacher to maximize time on task; teachers are expected to make the most of every moment, directing concentration toward intended learning outcomes. Emerging digital platforms extend the promise of such thinking.

The full effects of this revolution are only starting to emerge as skillful designers of instruction work to build upon the already impressive array of digitally accessible offerings that learners now, often freely, draw upon. At its best, perhaps, learners are confronted with a vast open landscape of manipulable space with which to fashion asynchronous learning experiences—that is, learning from teachers whose activity is not simultaneous with their own—wherever and whenever they choose. In place of teachers establishing the setting, attending to the pace, mood and configuration of the classroom, these traditional responsibilities of teaching would now rest entirely on the shoulders of the learner. For the optimum, seamless learning experience, the goal becomes how best to calibrate educational delivery to the rhythm of the concrete, everyday life of family, work, and play.

This is where the virtual teacher comes in. What needs to be managed now is a matter of instructional design, now digitally optimized to certain educational needs and interests. The designer, increasingly incorporating the use of algorithms that gather student input data to

---

[8] For a version of this, see Allen Collins and Richard Halverson, *Rethinking Education in the Age of Technology: The Digital Revolution and Schooling in America*, 2nd edn. (New York: Teachers College Press, 2018).

make ongoing, fine-grained adjustments to each student's situation, can effectively narrow the scope of learning. Data-driven instruction thereby sidesteps many of the distractions, inconsistencies, and human foibles of traditional teaching settings. In doing so, instructional designers bend and even subvert the elements of teaching. The "teacher's" cares are reduced to clearly indicated, efficiently organized outcomes presumed to be relevant to the learner; authority becomes something impersonal, namely the system itself with its designer out of sight; the virtues displayed are severely constricted in scope; and the interpretation of subject matter, the enactment of judgment, and the articulation of purpose are all calibrated to meet the particular instrumental objectives being pursued. No frills, no pretenses, just efficient, replicated transactions designed to advance the student toward specified goals. And as for the sense of place, the virtual learning site can be gone in a swipe or click.

It may come as a relief to learn that technological innovations do not necessarily spell the doom of teaching. Given the essential role of teaching in sustaining and renewing all forms of cultural life, it is unlikely that the need for teachers will disappear anytime soon. Revolutions in printing and the expansion of literacy liberated many from the grips of church and state by creating a way to transfer knowledge without dependence on teachers. But this revolution also led to a higher demand for teachers. It turns out that to take full advantage of a library or participate in complex cultural practices, one must have already established the necessary kinds of capacities and commitments, skills and knowledge that your prior teachers have provided.[9] It isn't a stretch to say that McKenzie and Madison find themselves in a position to take advantage of educational resources around them precisely because of the vital role teachers have played in their lives.

---

[9] Kentaro Toyama makes a similar point, among others, in his critique of our blind faith in technology to solve educational problems. Kentaro Toyama, *Geek Heresy: Rescuing Social Change from the Cult of Technology* (New York: PublicAffairs, 2015).

Who can say how teaching and education will change, or the degree to which we can sidestep teachers and bend time and place to maximize learning? There is no lack of commentaries that point to the kinds of waste now incurred in this vast enterprise. But neither is there an end in sight where satisfying kinds of teaching carry on. What MacKenzie and Madison bring into view is perhaps not the wholesale replacement of traditional kinds of classrooms, but a new perspective on how such settings and the kinds of ends they serve should be understood and managed. The question is whether something is lost in the process of becoming quicker and more efficient at overcoming the traditional constraints of time and space in teaching, dissipating the sense of place.

Rethinking the Place of Teaching

Throughout most of human history teaching has been situated in places saturated with meaning associated with ongoing practice, as with the carpenter and apprentice noted earlier. The character of the place for teaching is bound up in the work itself, and the practice that it continues. The modern institution of schooling somewhat complicates this picture. Still, it goes without saying that the modern school has established itself as a distinctive place, invested with a panoply of real and imagined emotions, sights, sounds, smells, and experiences. The school is not just a physical building with walls and classrooms, it also encompasses the collective interactions of people, objects, and ideas, cultural conflict, the creation and reproduction of values, norms and prejudices, and much more. Schools are unavoidably entangled in deep patterns of social injustice, but serve also as public sites where such patterns may be observed, criticized, and in some cases overcome in ways that foster worthwhile social interaction of many kinds. Against that background, the effort of teachers to create a place conducive to the good they hope to achieve is undeniably challenging. What is at stake, at the granular level, is the way teachers think about and act upon their particular settings of practice.

Perhaps more is at stake than we recognize. Albert Borgmann, a theorist of technology, worries that too strong of a reliance on technologies of escape or convenience can undermine cultural traditions (or what he calls *focal practices*) that depend on bringing people together, renewing relational bonds, reaffirming commitments, and engaging in meaningful experiences of value beyond what is merely instrumental for some specific purpose.[10]

To see what he means, consider his example of the family meal.[11] There are all sorts of families of course. But whether one is a single parent who shares dinner with a child or a member of an extended group of family and friends who assemble together for a special occasion, the family meal draws from a rich, established context of traditions and things. The dining table, the home-cooked meal, the dinner conversation all enrich and are enriched by traditions of food preparation, local/family customs and habits, and the personalities of participants. The various roles and relationships and the physical (not virtual) presence of family members not only require their engagement but also serve to bring out certain potentialities of talent, virtue, and personality.

There are many inconvenient aspects to this tradition—it takes time and skill to make a meal, and the quality of a home-cooked meal is not always predictable (or good). Often the last thing you want to do at the end of the day is talk to your kids, spouse, or baby brother. And nothing is catered to your immediate wants—you can't eat anything you want, listen to the music you want, or escape mind-numbing questions like, "How was your day?"

Moreover, what is gained from this focal practice often escapes our immediate notice; its value cannot be neatly determined and standardized. Not only do participants bring to the table different roles,

---

[10] Albert Borgmann, *Technology and the Character of Contemporary Life: A Philosophical Inquiry* (Chicago: University of Chicago Press, 2009), 196–210.

[11] Borgmann, *Technology and the Character of Contemporary Life*, 196–210.

experiences, and degrees of appreciation, but also the meaning and effects of coming together from week to week broaden and deepen over time as it becomes a part of the participants' collective and individual identities. A child who doesn't understand why everyone must eat their meal together, possibly even without cell phones, may have to wait until she has a child of her own before she can fully appreciate the value of intimate moments spent with her family. Simply put, in order to participate in focal practices, one must tolerate any number of inconvenient and unpredictable obstacles. It takes work to get the benefits. You must be *present*, situated in a distinct place.

Unlike the "ubiquity and instantaneity of commodities" that help us escape the inconvenience of it all—think of McDonalds—focal practices are distinguished by their *fullness of presence* and "moments of completeness." Borgmann writes,

> Working out on a Stairmaster while watching a mountain valley on a plasma screen and talking to your partner via a Bluetooth headset seems to procure everything you can have on a walk in the Rattlesnake Valley with your spouse—except the commanding presence of the here and now.[12]

This *commanding presence of the here and now* endows the family meal with a quality that can't be reduced to its nutritional content or its functional role in teaching children table manners and the rules of polite conversation. The same *might* be true about the setting of a classroom, especially when considering the nature of presence (as we will see in the chapter that follows). There is something to be said for the way some teachers unmistakably succeed in creating a sense of focal practice: students and teacher gathering together for large blocks of time, sensing their meaningful presence together within the established features of the setting, the place they share. As with the established focal practice of a meal being more than its nutritional results, many

---

[12] Albert Borgmann, "The Here and Now: Theory, Technology, and Actuality," *Philosophy & Technology* 24, no. 1 (2011): 16.

classrooms are places that do much more than produce academic results of some kind.

The analogy can be taken a step further. We are engulfed today with nutritional details in a culture that is in danger of losing (or has it already lost) its way with regard to healthy, communal ways of eating. Similarly, the very idea of creating satisfying places for teaching and learning is in danger of being eclipsed by ways of thinking centered upon uniform, often measurable details. In contemporary culture, many people (not least of all school administrators and policy makers) focus on bottom-line results of one kind or another, the outputs of the system. Qualitative aspects of the experience of being in an educational setting are inherently difficult to grasp, comprehend, or evaluate. It is tempting to favor convenience and efficiency over quality and the hard work it entails. Recall our mention in the preface of "avoiding parking hassles" as a notable reason given by one institution to take their online classes. Moreover, there are certainly times when one can learn useful things more easily online than face-to-face in a classroom while also avoiding the inconvenience of having to go and be there.

Still, we contend that something essential is missed when we reduce teaching to its immediate instrumental value. Like the family meal, teaching occurs within a thickly textured physical, social, and linguistic environment. Whether standing around a workbench of a shop, sitting in a leaky, decrepit classroom, or gathered together around a handcrafted hardwood table in an elite boarding school, the physical space of teaching ascribes meaning to what is being taught. But importantly, the physical space and furnishings do not exhaust the possibilities where the sense of place is concerned. Rich decor does not necessarily generate the sense of a place's meaningfulness, and the lowliest of settings where teaching takes place can be infused with the sense of being a place of extraordinary value and significance. The sense of place is a creation of those involved, making what they will of the circumstances.

Time is a factor in creating the sense of place as well. As many teachers recognize, just as we fail to appreciate the rich textures of place when we reduce it to its spatial dimensions, we flatten the fullness of time when we dismiss its qualitative character. Think again of the subjective experiences likely to be derived from McKenzie's and Madison's frenetic style of learning, driven by a fast-paced and efficiently measured utilization of time. What are they racing for? Are there learning experiences that gestate slowly, things to engage with—and that perhaps can only be engaged with—in a more contemplative frame of mind? Some teachers relish the pauses and occasionally slow down the pace for very good reasons. The sense of place is partly a product of some shared notions about the value of time spent well together.

It is precisely here, in fact, that the age-old challenge of establishing the place of teaching opens up extraordinary new opportunities— to say nothing of the new challenges they involve. For the kinds of technologically mediated learning now emerging can and often do become vital parts of the classroom settings that teachers must learn to manage well. It is a cliché that the young know more about emergent technologies than their teachers do, but being *immersed* in new technologies is not the same thing as *using them well*. Recall the vital role of teachers with respect to virtue and care, forms of understanding, practical wisdom, and educational purpose. McKenzie and Madison will struggle to find these in the constricted parameters of virtual teaching. We cannot predict how skillful teachers will incorporate new technologies in richly satisfying places of learning, but this will be an increasingly important issue for teachers to address.

The Problems of Place

Whatever the promise of liberated learning, there is something to say for time spent in the more or less well-managed settings of practice. One learns how to *be* in such settings, and to think about the way their inherent constraints impact us for good or ill. It is worth dwelling a moment on just what it is one learns.

All teaching is dressed up in ideals and good intentions, and everywhere teachers also fall short. The compound of elements makes this inevitable. Things sometimes do come together in deeply satisfying ways, but over time teaching is more accurately described as a catalog of partial successes and frequent misfires. Given the inherent problematic nature of teaching, this is to be expected. And yet, it is not news that somehow many teachers make a real difference in the lives of (at least some of) their students. This speaks to why place matters in teaching. Sustained experience together gives teachers and students needed time and space to sort things out and discover what is possible.

This is where the creative activity of establishing a sense of place is a vital element of teaching. The physical setting provides the raw materials those present encounter, but places are also made and sustained by way of what transpires there. As the elements of practice come into play, the setting becomes a place that can either augment or diminish the quality of experience of those involved. To some extent, this does involve active efforts to design suitable and appealing arrangements of the space and things within it, desks, chairs, other furnishings. But significantly, establishing the sense of place centers on how those involved there come to make it a distinctive place of their own, a place to belong, feel secure, and possibly to flourish.

Not all places attain such a positive sense. Indeed, schooling is entirely capable of conveying and reinforcing harsh lessons of injustice and managing student populations in ways that are punishing and counterproductive. Tragically, some students are best described as in fact being confined, put in their place. For many critics, the compulsory nature of schools and its rigid timetables and rules for walking in hallways have a pernicious influence on learning, offering students the bitter taste of coercion and the stifling of their intellectual curiosity and freedom. The ways school settings are managed leave deep marks—of privilege and difference, fitness and deviance, worth and marginality— that can last a lifetime. These profound concerns warrant unrelenting attention.

The taken-for-granted reality of schooling makes it easy to forget that universal education is a singular and relatively recent achievement in human history. What makes the expansion of public education more remarkable is that it proceeded in a manner that successfully resisted, at least until recently, the full force of market logic and commodification that dominates most aspects of life today. It remains to be seen what becomes of the institution of schooling on a global scale in this respect. As the historian of education Diane Ravitch observes, corporate interests, often aligned with technological innovations of the kind we have already noted, may very well alter the landscape of public education for the worse.[13] The situation is fluid and it isn't clear what opportunities teachers will have in the years ahead to create the kind of place for their work that they would wish to establish, or what schooling itself, as a distinctive place apart, will become.

What is clear is that far more than simply a designated space and time for skill acquisition and information transfer, schools have remained places of community pride, places set aside for children to participate in the drama of growing up. The saliency of this period in life is not lost to the purveyors of popular culture; memories of our own school experiences inevitably intersect with images of school life portrayed in popular culture—the archetypes of the heroic, the caring, and the apathetic teacher or student, the graffiti-ridden and loud halls of the inner-city school, and the imposing even suffocating halls of the college preparatory. Clichés and all, the school represents a prominent place in the lives of most participants and serves as a powerful public reminder of the uniqueness and vitality of the communities that build and sustain them.

Hannah Arendt provides perhaps the most compelling defense of schools as *places apart*.[14] Schooling, for her, is a rite of passage into adulthood. Teachers are responsible for initiating the young into the

---

[13] Diane Ravitch, *Reign of Error: The Hoax of the Privatization Movement and the Danger to America's Public Schools* (New York: Random House, 2013).

[14] Arendt, "The Crisis in Education," 188–89.

public world, so that they, in turn, can take their place in society and renew the world in unforeseeable ways. As places apart, schools occupy a critical, intermediate space between the world of children and the world of adults, between the private sphere and the public sphere. It is a place apart from all others because children must step outside the small, intimate and confining space of their home in order to prepare for the diverse and complex demands of public citizenship and life. At the same time, they must also be shielded from premature exposure to the unforgiving glare of the public limelight, and the quick and easy escape into consumer culture and technology.

Which brings us back to the teacher. In this intermediate space of schooling as a place apart, teachers must establish what their particular settings of practice will be like. Being there, what answers will students find for the obvious questions: What is this place for? Do I belong here? What does this place expect of or bring out in me? For teachers, equally pressing questions concern the sense of place they would hope to establish, a deeply challenging task. Most teachers strive to get it right, but in matters of this kind, there is no simple roadmap. Set apart from the rest of life, the place may prove to be good both as a place to be and as a place that prepares one for what is to come. But as all teachers know, every setting where teaching takes place can become as well a site of frustration and derailed hopes for those involved.

Why Place Matters

Think of the places you want to be in. Some of them may be places to visit, but the ones that matter most are places you would wish to be in, in some fuller, more satisfying sense—places of activity and engagement, of community and belonging. Anyone with the means can buy a ticket that gets you someplace to visit or pass through, but those more settled and satisfying places require more of a person. Typically, they demand both a good deal of time and the readiness to be there that comes from a developed capacity to meaningfully engage in places of learning and cooperative activity. What basic capacities must one develop before one can even conceive of developing the specialized capacities needed to cook or repair motorcycles, read texts with care or solve complex problems, ski or sing? At all levels of such personal development, teachers are often the caretakers of those places where we sense that we do belong or might belong and learn to take part.

The role of teachers is not just to develop certain skills and student interests. It is also to establish a setting that enhances the very capacity of students to form and sustain interests. We all must learn how to hang in there when things are difficult, recognize that despite the often frustrating complexity of social settings, it can be worthwhile to persist and engage with others in more or less worthwhile ways. This may be more important now than ever, given the range of distractions our devices put so near at hand, often taking us from the place we happen to be. Place has become a more fragile thing. So it matters to what extent teachers today, in concert with their students, create a sense of place infused for a time with meaning.

Thinking about your own experience teaching and being taught

- Considering the variety of settings and different senses of place you have experienced, from the liberating and transformative to the constraining and even oppressive, how does one's sense of place shape the educational experience? What accounts for the impact?
- What role have you seen teachers play in creating the conditions for certain settings to become distinctly a place apart?

Thinking about conceptions and theories of place in teaching

- Compare virtual places of teaching to traditional face-to-face places. Does the difference matter?
- What do you make of Borgmann's analysis of technology and its potential problems? Can teaching be a focal practice in his sense of the term? Why or why not?

Thinking about how place relates to the other elements of teaching

- Where teaching takes place, all the elements of teaching come into play; how important is the place itself in how the various elements emerge and play out?
- Are there particular elements that seem most clearly affected by or related to the establishing of a strong sense of place in practice?

Thinking about place in other contexts of life

- In what ways should educational settings today draw upon or respond to the pace and characteristics of technologically driven social and cultural change?
- Given the nature of digital culture today, are traditional school settings—maintaining the sense of a place apart—still necessary? And if so, what is the teacher's role in creating them?

8

Engaged Presence

The account of a day in the life of a substitute teacher:

I collected the synonym-and-antonym worksheets. The last task of the day was for me to read to the class from Danny the Champion of the World, by Roald Dahl, starting from where Mrs. Browning had left off, at the beginning of chapter two. I read to them about the BFG, the Big Friendly Giant, who catches children's dreams in glass bottles and makes magic powders out of them. "A dream," I read, "as it goes drifting through the night air, makes a tiny little buzzing humming sound, a sound so soft and low it is impossible for ordinary people to hear it. But the BFG can hear it easily." I looked up. The whole class was motionless. Carlton's head was up; Ian's head was up; Nash's head was up; the tattletale girls were all intent on hearing every word I was saying. Everyone was listening. I kept going. I got to the part where the Big Friendly Giant uses a long blowpipe to blow his dream powders into children's rooms. The sleeping child breathes in the powder, and begins dreaming a marvelous dream. "Then the magic powder really takes over—and suddenly the dream is not a dream any longer but a real happening—and the child is not asleep in bed—he is fully awake and is actually in the place of the dream and is taking part in the whole thing." I reached the end of the chapter. "Wow," I said. "Should I read some more?"

"YES," said the class. It was the first time they'd spoken in unison since they'd said "I will be the best I can be" at the beginning of the day. I read the next chapter, which was about kite flying. It was good, but not quite as good as the bit about blowing pipes and dreams, and some kids got squirmy, but still, they listened.

Nicholson Baker, *Substitute*[1]

---

[1] Nicholas Baker, *Substitute: Going to School with a Thousand Kids* (New York: Blue Rider Press, 2016), 52.

Nicholas Baker brought a writer's eye to the various classrooms he worked in for a while as a substitute teacher, presenting himself as the teacher wherever he was assigned for the day. The students made their presence known to him as well, as you would expect. Following that morning ritual of declaring themselves ready to be their best, they spent their time just being themselves. A certain chaotic bustling was the hallmark of the day, structured around the work and routines laid out for everyone to follow. The reading Baker describes here dramatically altered the experience of being there together for Baker and the students alike. The change is revealing.

One thing it reveals is a central fact about teaching, the unpredictable reality of how the experience of teaching and being taught hinges on the ways in which teachers and students become present to one another. This is the element of engaged presence. In Baker's account, he acknowledges how limited and forgettable his engagement with those particular students was for most of the day; he was probably equally forgettable to them. The quality of engagement in teaching is a state of affairs, but it is a state that is changeable, fluid, and dynamic. Suddenly, as he read about the BFG, the room was motionless, heads were up, everyone was listening. As some kids started to squirm, you can imagine it would change again. The point, though, is the unavoidable particularity of teaching; that being present to one another as teacher and students is in itself meaningful in various, often subtle, sometimes deeply consequential ways. As an element of teaching, a great deal turns on the quality of engaged presence.

It is worth noting that while every other element involves some doing—which we have signaled by way of words like enacting, conveying, rendering, and so on—engaged presence has everything to do with being there; it concerns how particular teachers and students connect with each other in the place where they find themselves drawn together. This does not mean that teachers (or students for that matter) do not act in ways that impact the quality of engaged presence. But to do so, the route is through the other elements. Engaged presence is, in effect, the product of how all the elements come together in a given place and time. This is why the quality of engagement is as fluid as it is—all those action verbs of teaching, enacting, displaying, judging, and so on as the elements resolve in some kind of engaged presence. As we see in the two phases of Baker's day, the experience of engaged presence is always subject to change.

In this chapter, we concentrate first on the question of how it happens that the elements of teaching come together in practice, creating the conditions of engaged presence. We suggest a number of considerations helpful in thinking about the quality of such experiences, and why engaged presence is in many respects the most elusive and challenging of the elements of teaching. We turn then to the notion of presence itself, and consider two ways to think about why it matters in teaching and in our lives. Enduring presence comes into view as a way to understand why teaching matters in the end.

The Nature of Engaged Presence

As Baker's day began, he was a stranger to the students in the class. Stepping up as their teacher, however, his mere physical presence as a stranger shifts in the direction of engaged presence with those particular students. All understand that they are in some sense answerable to one another: there are certain, perhaps rather vague, expectations and responsibilities that flow in both directions.

The mere fact of being physically present with others does not constitute engaged presence. To sense the shift Mr. Baker makes, you might think of it this way. Riding on a bus with strangers does not require your engaged presence. But if it is a school bus carrying a teacher and her class on a field trip, that's a different matter. All are engaged in a common project, this trip, but more importantly, they all recognize their mutual obligations to attend to one another. Minimally, the students are mindful of the teacher's monitoring gaze, while the teacher knows to keep an eye on whether the students are behaving appropriately. They share some sense of engaged presence.

As a form of activity, teaching always generates such a sense. Think of it in the broadest terms as what it feels like to be in the presence, not of *a* teacher or student, but of *your* teacher or student. The "your" indicates some degree of *engaged* presence. The relationships of teaching are subject to change, in a heartbeat, though we all have experienced (we suspect) how stable many experiences with teachers have been in our lives; a tone is sometimes established early on in a course or school year with a teacher that seems scarcely to change day in and day out (for better or worse). Other prolonged experiences of engaged presence are mercurial, unpredictable. To some extent this has to do with the personalities of all concerned, and their expectations in the situation. But that is not very helpful, for the question is how the experiences in and of teaching, the actual quality of engaged presence in particular settings, come about. That, after all, is what matters. We noted earlier that engaged presence is a product of all the elements of teaching coming together in some way. But how do the elements combine in practice?

How the Elements Combine

Let's step back and think for a moment about the very idea of teaching. In the most general terms, what does it mean to teach anyone anything? Think of the examples of teaching you recalled at the beginning of this book, and then allow your memory and imagination to suggest a few more. Whatever examples you dwell upon, consider the engaged presence involved, the way that both the ones teaching and the ones being taught are answerable to and aware of each other's presence in those roles. Each is more or less engaged in what is understood to be a teaching situation, which is why their mutually responsive presence matters.

Often, it is true, teaching situations include students (and at times possibly even teachers) who are or become disengaged. Is engaged presence something one chooses? It is entirely possible to opt out altogether; some students do, and in the case of teachers, burnout is the term employed for those headed in that direction or already there.

But notice that in most teaching situations, when those involved drift off and daydream, or drool on the desk, with a nudge or a start they return to the reality of the teaching situation in which they are (perhaps dreamily) present to take part in. The nudge or wake-up call returns them to the state of the (at least minimally) engaged presence called for by the situation. Most of us, most of the time, tend to answer that call to presence; we are in some sense answerable to one another in settings of teaching, mutually responsive *as* teacher and student.

Being (more or less) engaged in a teaching situation means taking part in a distinct form of social activity involving the elements we have presented. We have teased them apart, but in experience they are woven together, becoming part of the fabric of the teaching situation. One's experience of that "fabric" is usually not the experience of, say, authority being exercised, or purposes identified, and so on, but of something simpler that binds the elements together. The teacher and student relate with one another for a time, focused on something that matters to them. Teaching resides in that medium of relationship and attention, our deeply human capacity to cooperate and put our heads together in a shared experience.

This is the stuff that the elements of teaching are made of. All of the elements arise from our being able to sustain cooperative relationships for a time focused on some project or shared intentions. The elements separately depend on that capacity, but then they combine to extend and develop that capacity through the teaching of everything human beings conceive of to teach. The experience of engaged presence results from this, becoming, in effect, the element that registers what the teaching means for those involved in the present situation.

A Case in Point

An example will help us here. Let's take the example of Sophie, an avid and wide-ranging reader, someone who now as an adult reads all kinds of things for work, pleasure, and increased clarity about the world. Along the way to being such a reader, she had teachers at three stages of her life who stand out in her mind for their influence on her being the kind of reader she is now. So we might say, tentatively, that Sophie would readily agree to the notion that the experience of engaged presence quite vividly applies to her experience with and of these teachers. She feels they changed her life. In those settings, she was all there and recalls them being there as her teachers just as fully.

Recounting her experiences in detail is not something we can do here; instead we will sketch these three extended examples of engaged presence and note all the other elements of teaching that were in play. At age six, Sophie says, she was struck by the way her teacher seemed to relish certain books; but she cared as well about Sophie's experience of those books, and we might say the object of care was the pleasure of bringing the books alive for Sophie and others. Being only six, whatever instruction she needed in order to learn how to read is now recalled in terms of how enticing it seemed to be able to read. Her teacher's judgment about the help she needed, correcting errors, reading aloud, and other matters provided Sophie with challenges she could handle. From early on, the classroom with its array of books and a reading corner and other decorative features felt welcoming to her, and dovetailed with her teacher's kindness and equanimity. She sensed that school was important, and her teacher reinforced inclinations to be attentive and purposeful. There were of course rules to follow and the usual array of noises, distractions, interruptions, but her teacher never seemed to her to be overwhelmed or overbearing, maintaining instead a steady, nurturing control of things as the year unfolded. By the end of it, she was reading her first chapter books.

At thirteen, Sophie was a capable reader, but she had been languishing in school. Her early enchantment was gone; most reading now was work. Her teachers for a couple of years had mostly leaned on her to read, if at all, just to accomplish assigned tasks. She wasn't reading at home, either. Her new language arts teacher didn't seem promising at first, a somewhat chilly and imposing figure. He seemed rather cold and demanding, always calling attention to following the rules, being on task. They were reading a play to start the year; initially Sophie was keeping up with the reading but it was dull. Things changed, though, dramatically. The teacher had students read certain lines, then pressed them to read them again, more expressively; he asked questions of a kind Sophie wasn't used to, questions that set her back, made her think, drew her out. Other students were drawn out, and drawn in together, as they talked about what the play, and the characters in it, were all about. This was different; the way they were now interacting turned the dull classroom space into a place she hadn't been in before. She would leave with questions that carried into the next day. She noticed the teacher's tact and skill in these discussions, his insights into the themes of the play, and began to sense how important it was to him that the students think about the details in the play, and how those related both to the work as a whole and to larger issues she thought about in her own life. Sometimes, the teacher's uncompromising ways would emerge: Sophie worried about being subject to his criticism as she engaged in the course. But in these circumstances, that feeling just fed her determination to push farther into the places her reading was taking her.

By twenty, Sophie was a university student in the humanities. She knew how to do well in courses, but had become somewhat uncertain about where it was leading. Success in schoolwork is satisfying up to a point, but it cannot be the point, at least it couldn't be for her much longer. Without a lot of thought about it, she signed up for a course in the English department on nonfiction writers. Her teacher made her purpose clear; she wanted these students to read with purposes of their own about crucial issues in the world. The subject matter reflected her judgment about stellar examples of nonfiction writing that exposes problems and awakens public attention to them. Sophie's experience with reading of this kind was limited, but the first texts affected her deeply, and she became intrigued to understand both how such work is done and where this kind of writing might take her. Her teacher was an astute judge of powerful writing, and convinced of its importance in view of the problems in the world she cared deeply about. This orientation was initially startling to Sophie, but she admired the teacher's clarity and confidence in speaking about her approach and why it mattered. Unlike the usual classroom spaces to which she was accustomed, this room seemed more charged, animated. There was a different sense of purpose there and she felt latent traits in her personality surfacing, aspirations to act on her sense of justice, the desire to speak truth to power. The act of reading had shifted for her once again, and her reading opened new horizons of possibility and understanding.

Thinking about This Case

The brief narrative linking these three experiences of engaged presence in Sophie's life seems like a happy story, but a number of points need to be emphasized in making sense of it. They fall into two sets, with an interlude in-between.

First, we used the example of reading in Sophie's life, but it could as well have been mathematics or dance, the sciences or history, music or motorcycle maintenance. Certain encounters of engaged presence with teachers are pivotal in developing our capacity to relate with others and attend to things that matter to us over time.

Second, given the first point, we should be clear that we do not mean to endorse Sophie's story as "the way it should be." The blossoming of reading in her life is not superior to, say, the blossoming of cooking in the life of someone who loves to cook. And similarly, the kind of teaching the scenario portrays is not intended as a model of what "good teaching is" or as the "best practice." Our view is that the notion of "best practice" in teaching should always be treated with a great deal of skepticism, for reasons that we hope are clear by now.

Third, we expect that you see that all the elements are incorporated in each of the scenes presented, for they are all evident. If we could elaborate in more detail, much more could be said about the ways is which authority was enacted, place was established, judgments were rendered and all the rest. Where space is short, your imagination can fill in the picture, based upon your own extensive experiences of engaged presence (and of course the features of these various elements that we have introduced in earlier chapters).

Fourth, the elements do not appear sequentially, nor do they all carry equal weight at any given time. Any of them might be foregrounded initially, or dominate the proceedings for a time. Sophie's experience was not the result of some formula or method for the ways the elements combined; things came together for her in fruitful ways that weren't, and likely could not have been, predictable or under anyone's control (though all of the teachers, in their distinctive approaches to teaching, surely would have anticipated generating satisfying responses of various kinds from some or even most of their students).

But let's pause a moment in order to flip the script. We offer the example of Sophie to suggest the ways in which our diverse experiences of engaged presence take form and develop as they do by virtue of the way that the elements of teaching combine in particular situations of life. The element of engaged presence is just the effect of such combining, the way care, authority, judgment, and so on play out together in actual, lived circumstances. For Sophie, at least where her love of reading was concerned, things played out well, overall. But notice four more things (since these contrast in tone, let's call them A, B, C, and D).

A. Sophie's story centers on three teachers encountered during the span of fourteen years. How often was her engaged presence with teachers, even where reading was concerned, experienced as a kind of drudgery compared to the times we highlighted? Much of that may have been due to other more or less useful kinds of learning and experiences, but often her teachers would have seen to her reading, given her assignments, tested her comprehension, offered reading suggestions, and so on, in ways that seemingly fell flat. Keep this in mind, however. Much of that work may have been vitally important in setting the stage for those more memorable peak experiences we have recounted. We just don't know enough about Sophie or the circumstances. More than that, teachers generally do not know how the capacities they hope to develop in their students may one day provide the basis for developments that change their lives.

B. Sophie was not the only student in any of the classes we describe. Things went "right" for her, but she sat alongside students for whom, conceivably, nothing went right: the storytelling was boring, the teacher was way too intrusive and pushy in discussions of the play (which was itself a drag), and the social justice warrior-professor was arrogant in ways that undermined her own commitments, at least in the eyes of Sophie's classmates. Every effort to get things right can succeed and fail at the same time, it would seem. And if that is so, how much happily engaged presence is necessary to justify the engaged presence of those suffering through the experience? What if it is the teacher who suffers? And most importantly, what if the difference between those whose engaged presence is by and large uplifting, and those for whom it is not, hints at, or screams of, prejudice of one kind or another?

C. One risk of a brief scenario like Sophie's is the loss of nuance. We see the elements playing out together in a way that has a powerful effect on Sophie, and one imagines every judgment the teacher makes, each authoritative gesture, and everything involved across the range of elements just folds in neatly. Nonsense. Sophie might remember it that way, just as you might remember certain experiences of engaged presence in your life as a time when everything just came together perfectly. The experienced reality is more complicated than what we are inclined to remember.[2] Sophie's teachers were fallible human beings working in the inherently complicated domain of a teacher's work. Their judgments were sometimes flawed, their virtues abandoned them from time to time, they lost sight of their cares and became muddled as to the purposes of what was happening at times; and let's face it, sometimes the subject matter just doesn't really matter or make sense. The place may still have been comfortable and welcoming, but in truth it was sometimes a bit confining or even oppressive.

D. Finally, there is a crucial component of time implicit in this story. Sophie's arc of experience in becoming an avid reader extended for years, but even these pivotal experiences stretched out over extended time periods—a school year or the length of a university course. Telling her

---

[2] See Daniel Kahneman, *Thinking Fast and Slow* (New York: Farrar, Straus and Giroux, 2011), 377–91.

story, the teachers seem to drop into place, sort of like Mr. Baker does. But in fact, it took time to establish the patterns of engaged presence that impacted her life. Even if Sophie can identify specific pivotal moments in her education, such moments occurred within a larger context of many other less memorable moments that prepared the way. Sophie's teacher at age six formed strong relational bonds by displaying kindness, joy, and care in multiple situations, while Sophie's teacher who asked probing questions about the play must somehow have earned the respect of students to elicit the serious responses that he did. Even at the university level, Sophie's judgments about the trustworthiness, character, and purposes of the professor, among other considerations bearing upon her experience in the course, would have needed time for Sophie to arrive at the point where this felt so right for her to engage in wholeheartedly.

In getting it "right" in the ways that Sophie's teachers did for her, they got a lot wrong; misfires happen, every element involves more ways to be faulty than fortuitous. In fact, however, right and wrong are judgments after the fact. The reality of the situations that seem to have been pivotal is much more complicated. The density of what is actually experienced in teaching situations matters in ways that this narrative account fails to address. Engaged presence is not just about what's "right" or what "works." Teaching in this way emerges from one's earliest experience of caregiving adults, loving family members and others with whom the first experiences of engaged presence took place—think of Sophie the toddler in her parent's lap, reading a book over and over again. As teachers, like parents, know, it is easy when everything goes right. Much of what really matters takes place when, as is more common, things are not entirely as everyone would like.

Two Views of Presence in Teaching

Sophie has spent some 15,000 hours in the company of teachers. This time together with teachers, what we are calling engaged presence, contributed to her becoming the kind of reader she now is. No doubt,

Sophie could identify other clear accomplishments she owes in part to her teachers. While she might struggle to spell these out, she can spell. Indeed, what would be easier for her would be to list many of the things, like spelling, which her teachers aimed to help her accomplish; there were always goals in view. The company of teachers revolves around the pursuit of certain ends, what we are here to learn or accomplish, usually reduced to what are we working on now.

Take a moment to put Sophie's 15,000 hours in context. At the primary and secondary levels of schooling today, there are roughly one billion students working on one thing or another in the company of teachers.[3] Something on the order of one hundred million more are working with teachers in higher education, and this is to say nothing of all those spending time with teachers in adult education classes, corporate instructional programs, private lessons, and so on. Every day, this almost unimaginably vast enterprise takes place as teachers and students resume their more or less purposeful presence together.

How should we understand this? Two ways of thinking about this come readily to mind. Let's take them up in turn.

The Utility of Presence

The first view centers on the common thread in all those billions of hours spent in the company of teachers every day, namely, that it is about the ends being served. Teaching is a goal-oriented activity meant to serve some end or purpose; goals and their achievement are always in view when students and teachers are present to one another. The point of the activity is achieving those various ends, or at least making progress toward those ends. In the presence of teachers, Sophie achieved various milestones and in the end emerged as an accomplished reader. Along the way, she became aware of a wide range of other goals that her teachers helped her to recognize and strive to achieve.

[3]   David Baker, *The Schooled Society* (Palo Alto: Stanford University Press, 2014), 24.

This way of thinking about the time teachers and students spend in each other's company centers on the usefulness of that time together, what philosophers call its utility. We can refer to this as the *utility of presence*. To the extent one adopts this perspective, whether as a teacher, student, or interested observer or supervisor, one's presence in the settings of teaching is more or less useful. There is after all an "aboutness" of teaching that is directional, it is leading toward some end. Some of these ends are specific and easily measured, say learning to solve for x, while others are broader and more complicated, such as teaching antiracism or cultivating patriotism. But all can contribute to the perception that teaching is to be viewed primarily, if not solely, in terms of its instrumental value—the ends it serves.

With a utility mindset, once the clarity of ends is established, teachers are left with the straightforward task of optimizing the means toward the end. The kind of means-end rationality we spoke of earlier (Chapter 5) is highlighted in order to be as efficient as possible in achieving one's stated goals. This approach is often accompanied by a drive for uniformity, in that all the quirky characteristics of the teacher, students or the setting are seen through the lens of what they bring about. In other words, the quality of engaged presence and the elements are evaluated by their contribution to achieving intended outcomes. A sense of humor might keep spirits up during a tough stretch of work, but it has no place if it merely amuses or distracts. Taking time to get to know your students is applauded if, and only if, that is the most efficient way to get students to reach their goals. In fact, all the elements are instrumentalized this way to fit this means-ends logic.

As we saw in the previous chapter, this way of thinking has stimulated a great deal of activity and innovation in the domains of instructional design. One can design the teaching experience purely in terms of getting the intended results. Thus, every element in teaching is manipulated for this purpose. Take, for instance, the way in which "social presence" is defined and utilized by scholars of online education. Some define it as "a feeling of community, a personal attachment"[4] while others refer to it as the "ability of learners to project themselves as 'real' people."[5] In both cases, its value lies in its ability to increase student engagement and course appeal. As one scholar puts it, the aim is to increase the "cognitive presence" of students by rendering group interactions "enjoyable and personally fulfilling so that students will remain in the cohort of learners for the duration of the program."[6] Here, social presence is only considered for its instrumental value in bringing about the intended outcome. No attention is paid to the value of community itself.

This way of thinking has a potentially deep impact on the way presence is understood even in the most traditional settings of teaching. If it were our only way to think about the meaning and value of engaged presence, every teacher would be first and foremost an efficiency expert. Like engineers looking to streamline every process, teachers would strive to make engaged presence pay off and an ethic of efficiency would reign. But an alternative ethic is conceivable. In fact, this book has laid out the case for it. The alternative way of thinking turns on a more open-ended, holistically evaluative approach to our presence together in teaching.

Integrity of Presence

As with any goal-oriented activity, it is tempting to fixate on the results and the most efficient means of getting there. In some teaching contexts, a concerted focus on utility of presence makes perfect sense. Where the ends are clear and compelling, a commitment to figuring out the optimal way of spending one's time toward achieving these goals is quite reasonable, provided, of course, there aren't other, possibly

---

[4] Rena M. Palloff and Keith Pratt, *Building Online Learning Communities: Effective Strategies for the Virtual Classroom*, 2nd edn. (San Francisco: Jossey-Bass, 2007).

[5] D. Randy Garrison, Terry Anderson, and Walter Archer, "Critical Inquiry in a Text-Based Environment," *Internet and Higher Education* 2, no. 2–3 (2000): 87–105.

[6] Palloff and Pratt, *Building Online Learning Communities*, 89.

countervailing, goals that also warrant our attention. But teaching almost always complicates things in this way. The goals of teaching are varied and continually shifting, and the effects of teaching extend beyond the explicit goals in ways that are often unpredictable and far-reaching.

Even if we could clearly capture and consistently meet the explicit goals of teaching, there is something more to be said about the activity of teaching itself. Teaching is not only a goal-oriented activity but also a social activity with a variety of moving parts. The problematic nature of teaching demands that it be considered more holistically, in a manner that doesn't reduce the activity to its bare-bone utility. Just as sharing a meal isn't only about hitting one's daily nutritional targets, or playing a game isn't only about winning, the activity of teaching is greater than its calculated utility. This is true for any complex human activity. Indeed, time spent in engaged presence—those billions of hours every day—matters in all kinds of ways, including, but not reducible to, the more discernible results and accomplishments that emerge from such engagement.

We have attempted here to present teaching more comprehensively, in terms of an *integrity of presence*. This involves the effort to see teaching in relation to all the elements of which it is comprised, to see it whole. To view teaching from this perspective entails attention to, in the particular contexts of practice, the range of elements that comprise what takes place. The vast enterprise of teachers and students engaging with one another in practice every day weaves a fabric of experience in which those involved are present to one another in all the ways they take part. Whether good, bad, or indifferent, patterns of authority relations are woven into this fabric, as are conceptions of purpose. The place has meanings of many kinds, not least in the ways that it frames the diverse objects of care that come into play. Present to one another in complex social settings, virtues of many kinds are called for, displayed, and cultivated, while patterns of judgment are infused in everything that transpires. And yes, the subject matter, in which all kinds of more or less useful goals and ends are located, confronts all involved with notions and issues as to its meaning and value, what there is to know and do, and how to make sense of what one is engaged in.

Where utility of presence turns on judgments of usefulness—what all the time teachers and students spend together is useful for—integrity of presence poses a different question: how do we do justice to the inherent complexity and many kinds of significance teaching invariably involves? Questions about useful outcomes still matter of course, but they should not eclipse other vital considerations regarding the quality of engaged presence, how the elements of teaching hang together in practice over time and, in doing so, shape and color our lives.

Why Teaching Matters

We are in a better position to see now what we could only hint at in the Introduction. Put simply, by way of engaged presence, teaching has an *enduring presence* in our lives, both individually and with respect to the cultural traditions and practices it draws upon, sustains, and helps to renew. If it were only a matter of specific kinds of usefulness, we could say of teaching and teachers, thanks for the help, and get on with our lives. Many people are inclined to think of teaching in this way, as the work of those who set the stage for what really matters in life. Teachers are left behind as we pursue the projects of life that we could never have conceived of let alone undertaken were it not for those teachers we are ready to forget. As we have attempted to show in this book, however, teaching is much more at the center of things. Comprised of the elements we have explored, teaching is a form of activity that reaches into all parts of our life and culture.

This means, among other things, that teaching warrants ongoing, careful attention. If teaching were a fundamental set of techniques instrumental in getting certain kinds of useful knowledge, information, and know-how transmitted, the task would be to monitor the performance of teachers and optimize the methods of teaching. But given the complexity and significance of the elements involved, teaching is inherently challenging, contentious, and problematic. In the long hours, days, years of time spent where teaching takes place, each of the elements has an impact and together over time the effects are profound, for better or worse. Teaching matters far more than its identifiable and intended outcomes.

The reality is that teaching is deeply implicated, first of all, in the flourishing of individuals. It is the form of activity that, by way of its range of component elements, prepares the ground for the range of capacities and powers one needs to meaningfully engage in worthwhile activities of any kind, as we saw in the example of Sophie's reading. But of course, teaching is a form of activity that is entirely capable of foreclosing possibilities, excluding, limiting, or diminishing the prospects of individuals or even entire categories of people. In both respects, teaching is a deeply *human* form of activity through which both what is best in us and what is worst may find expression.

Teaching is also implicated in the flourishing of cultural traditions and diverse practices central to our lives. The traditions and practices we gravitate toward and, by learning to take part in, help to renew, could not survive the breakdown of teaching that would leave them defenseless. They survive and evolve over time and across generations owing to the wherewithal of teachers whose enduring presence is found in their continued existence. Here too, teaching is not associated only and always with traditions and practices of which we would all approve. Bull fighting and boxing, for example, are as dependent on teaching as are brain surgery or ballet.

In addition to the survival and continuance of cultural traditions and practices, the quality of teaching plays a role in their vitality and flourishing. Traditions and practices of all kinds can perhaps get by in a more or less healthy condition with some effort. They can also wither and become hollow when those who teach within or about them lose faith in their value or can't persuade others to care. Worse still, perhaps, would be if the most fundamental, generic capacities for active engagement in diverse but demanding activities were to become widely underdeveloped in the young. Conversely, cultural traditions and practices thrive when there are teachers who can pass on their passion and talents to others, or who demonstrate their cares about worthwhile forms of learning and activity of many kinds.

At the outset of this book, we suggested that teaching is an essential and inherently problematic form of human activity. We can now further suggest that this is why it matters how teaching and the work of teachers is viewed and understood. Given how critical teachers are for the flourishing of students and of cultural traditions and practices, and given also its problematic nature, teaching warrants the care and attention needed to see it for what it is, as best we can, in all its promising yet troublesome complexity. Teachers ought to think of their work in this way; it is a demanding, rewarding, and impactful practice to dwell upon and strive to do good work within. And teachers deserve for their work to be regarded by others—especially those who would manage, modify, or redirect it—in this more comprehensive way as well.

The enduring presence of teachers is certainly found in the recesses of individual memory; think for a moment of teachers who have had an abiding impact on your life. The impacts of teaching, however, extend much farther, ranging across all aspects of human culture and possibility. Yet many fail to see this clearly. It is rather odd that while schooling has emerged as a global institution, teaching is often treated as a managed resource, certain useful services broadly distributed. But we should all know better than to think strictly in those terms. Both in and outside of school settings, teachers are human beings working with other human beings in a place they inhabit together, interacting in ways that make sense to them in that place, pursuing the various more or less meaningful ends that those present see the point of pursuing. Given the teacher's role with respect to the elements involved in this sustained engagement, all kinds of things that have enduring significance transpire. Certain competencies, powers, and capacities develop; habits and patterns of focused attention strengthen; personal traits, dispositions, and interests become engrained; the scope of one's knowledge and know-how enlarges; ways of cooperating, interacting, and collaborating with others unfold; the sense of one's place, potential and possibilities in life clarifies.

The complex nature of the practice of teaching makes this so. In the end, for better or worse, teachers convert the challenges of engaged presence into the filaments of lasting influence. In doing so, the diverse experiences of teaching and being taught shape what we are capable of doing, learning, and ultimately becoming in our lives.

Thinking about your own experience teaching and being taught

- Consider the range of engaged presence in your experience of teaching or being taught. What is the relationship between the quality of engagement and the educational impact of those experiences?
- What forms of engaged presence has had the most enduring impact in your life? How so?

Thinking about conceptions and theories of presence in teaching

- What does it mean to say that it is in engaged presence that the elements of teaching combine?
- What accounts for the various kinds of enduring presence that teaching generates?

Thinking about how presence relates to the other elements of teaching

- The elements of teaching are all components of presence; how challenging is it to combine them in stable and desirable ways?
- From the standpoint of the teacher, are there elements of particular significance? What about from the standpoint of students?

Thinking about presence in other contexts of life

- In what ways does the enduring presence of teachers contribute in positive ways to one's life? Can such presence be a source of enduring harm?
- What human capacities are most clearly enhanced by way of one's engagement over time with teachers whose presence endures in one's life?

Epilogue

It is through being taught and teaching that, to a significant degree, we find our place in the world, and in relation to one another as well. It is by way of teaching that we develop much of the capacity we have to make sense of what we see and take part in. Our teachers mediate many of the ways the world becomes intelligible to us and often give flight to our imagination, even as they also present us with some of the harsher lessons of life.

It is by way of the elements of teaching that we all become witnesses to central features of our world and gain some sense of our own ways of participating in it. In the many places where we find ourselves in the presence of teachers, we encounter all of the elements of teaching as they play out in some way, for better or worse. What we learn of these things in such encounters resonates in all parts of our lives.

How we attend to the things that matter is the critical question of course. Today, at a quickening pace, devices in hand, the volume of information, ideas, attractions, points of view, knowledge and knowledge claims, distractions, appeals, threats, diverse peoples and endless forms of cultural expression—good, bad, and mystifying—are all more present and pressing than ever before. Will the experiences of teaching in our lives help us focus on the kinds of things that matter most? Or is teaching itself now in the process of being overwhelmed or reconfigured, perhaps beyond recognition?

We offer no answer. Still, the deep impacts of good teaching strike us as profoundly important today. Think of what the experiences of being taught can mean in settings where the elements of teaching play out in ways conducive to the flourishing of all involved. As Chris Higgins explains, the flourishing of teachers in their work is no small part of this; it is fundamental.[1]

---

[1]   Higgins, *The Good Life of Teaching*, 9–10.

This book is offered as a guide and not a prescription. In that spirit, we contend that each of us has a role to play in the kinds and quality of teaching that prevails. That means thinking about how best to advance the conditions that help teachers do well all the things that matter in their work. For our part, we would briefly suggest three general ways in which to support the good work and flourishing of teachers.

First, since teaching is inherently complex, the mindfulness and recognition of that complexity should be the starting place for anyone engaged either in teaching or in governing, evaluating, administering, or striving to influence the work of teachers. Short cuts and simplistic "solutions" are rarely successful and much more likely to generate unintended results and more confusion.

Second, since teaching is inherently contentious and problematic, the quality of deliberations in and about the work of teachers should be enhanced and ongoing. Those involved will need to prepare for and commit themselves to the demands of such efforts to think and act with discernment, care, and a charitable spirit that respects different points of view. This describes both the challenge and significance of serious, open-ended teacher education.

Finally, since teaching matters in a host of elemental ways, grounded in the particular situations of practice and engaged presence, the work of teachers should be accorded the respect it deserves and the breathing room of sufficient autonomy all teachers need to become and be their best in practice. This entails the room for and risk of teachers falling short in the many ways they might, but provides the needed foundation for the kinds of genuinely significant and enduring good that the practice of teaching makes possible.

Bibliography

"Academy Mission Statement." *Phillips Exeter Academy*. Accessed April 7, 2019. http://64.140.204.145/about_us/171_9259.aspx

Adams, John Truslow. "To 'Be' or to 'Do': A Note on American Education." *Forum LXXXI*, no. 6 (1886–1930): 321–27.

Allen, Danielle. *Education and Equality*. Chicago: University of Chicago, 2016.

Annas, Julia. *Intelligent Virtue*. Oxford: Oxford University Press, 2011.

Annas, Julia. "Phenomenology of Virtue." *Phenomenology and the Cognitive Sciences 7* (2008): 21–34.

Apple, Michael. *Ideology and Curriculum*. 4th edn. New York: Routledge, 2019.

Arendt, Hannah. "The Crisis in Education." In *Between Past and Future*. New York: Penguin Books, 1993.

Arendt, Hannah. *Eichmann in Jerusalem: A Report on the Banality of Evil*. New York: Penguin Classics, 2006 (1963).

Arendt, Hannah. *The Human Condition*. Chicago: University of Chicago Press, 1998 (1958).

Aristotle, *Nicomachean Ethics*. Oxford: Oxford University Press, 2009.

Armstrong, Karen. *Twelve Steps to a Compassionate Life*. New York: Anchor Books, 2010.

Ayers, William. *Teaching Toward Freedom: Moral Commitment and Ethical Action in the Classroom*. Boston: Beacon Press, 2005.

Baker, David. *The Schooled Society*. Palo Alto: Stanford University Press, 2014.

Baker, Nicholas. *Substitute: Going to School with a Thousand Kids*. New York: Blue Rider Press, 2016.

Baldwin, James. "A Talk to Teachers." In Baldwin: Collected Essays. New York: The Library of America, 1998.

Biesta, Gert. "How General Can *Bildung* Be? Reflections on a Future of a Modern Educational Ideal." *Journal of Philosophy of Education* 36, no. 3 (2002): 377–90.

Borgmann, Albert. *Technology and the Character of Contemporary Life: A Philosophical Inquiry*. Chicago: University of Chicago Press, 2009.

Borgmann, Albert. "The Here and Now: Theory, Technology, and Actuality." *Philosophy & Technology* 24, no. 1 (2011): 5–17.

Bourdieu, Pierre and Jean-Claude Passeron. *Reproduction in Education, Society and Culture*. 2nd edn. London: Sage Press, 2000.

Bowles, Samuel and Herbert Gintis. *Schooling in Capitalist America: Educational Reform and the Contradictions of Economic Life*. Chicago: Haymarket Books, 2011.

Brighouse, Harry. *On Education*. New York: Routledge, 2006.

Bynum, Sarah Shun-Lirn. *Ms. Hempel Chronicles*. Boston: Mariner Books, 2009.

Collins, Allen and Richard Halverson. *Rethinking Education in the Age of Technology: The Digital Revolution and Schooling in America*. 2nd edn. New York: Teachers College Press, 2018.

Crawford, Matthew. *Shop Class as Soulcraft*. New York: Penguin Press, 2000.

Darling, Linda, Audrey Amrein-Beardsley, Edward Haertel, and Jesse Rothstein, "Evaluating Teacher Evaluation." *The Phi Delta Kappan* 93, no. 6 (March 2012): 8–15.

Denby, David. *Lit Up: One Reporter. Three Schools. Two-Four Books That Can Change Lives*. New York: Henry Holt, 2016.

Dennett, Daniel. *Darwin's Dangerous Idea*. New York: Touchstone, 1995.

Deresiewicz, William. *Excellent Sheep: The Miseducation of the American Elite and the Way to a Meaningful Life*. New York: Free Press, 2015.

Dewey, John. *Experience and Education*. New York: Touchstone, 1997 (1938).

Dreyfus, Hubert L. and Stuart E. Dreyfus. "Expertise in Real World Contexts." *Organization Studies* 26, no. 5 (2005): 779–91.

Dreyfus, Hubert. *On the Internet*. New York: Routledge, 2001.

Dunne, Joseph. *Back to the Rough Ground: Practical Judgment and the Lure of Technique*. South Bend: University of Notre Dame, 2001.

Edmundson, Mark. *Why Football Matters: My Education in the Game*. New York: Penguin, 2014.

Egan, Kieran. *The Future of Education: Reimagining Our Schools from the Ground Up*. New Haven: Yale University Press, 2010.

Farber, Paul and Dini Metro-Roland. "The Promise and Limits of Online Learning: Reexamining Authority in the Classroom." In *Philosophy of Education 2011*, edited by Robert Kunzman. Urbana, IL: Philosophy of Education Society, 2012.

Farber, Paul and Dini Metro-Roland. "Being on One's Way: Place, Technology and the Moral Commodification of Education." In *Philosophy of Education 2013*, edited by Cris Mayo. Urbana, IL: Philosophy of Education Society, 2014.

Frankfurt, Harry. *The Reasons of Love*. New York: Princeton University Press, 2006.

Freire, Paulo. *Pedagogy of the Oppressed: 30th Anniversary Edition*. New York: Bloomsbury Academic, 2014.

Gadamer, Hans-Georg. *Truth and Method*. 2nd edn. New York: Bloomsbury Academic, 2013 (1975).

Garrison, Randy D., Terry Anderson, and Walter Archer. "Critical Inquiry in a Text-Based Environment." *Internet and Higher Education* 2, no. 2–3 (2000): 87–105.

Gordon, Mordechai and Maxine Greene, eds. *Hannah Arendt and Education: Renewing Our Common World*. New York: Perseus Press, 2001.

Greene, Maxine. *Releasing the Imagination: Essays on Education, the Arts and Social Change*. New York: Jossey-Bass, 1995.

Griffith, Mark. "Origins and Relations to the Near East." In *Ancient Education*. Oxford: John Wiley and Sons, 2015.

Hacking, Ian. *The Social Construction of What?* Cambridge: First Harvard University Press, 1999.

Hanh, Thich Nhat. *At Home in the World: Stories and Essential Teachings from a Monk's Life*. Berkeley: Parallax Press, 2016.

Hansen, David. *The Call to Teach*. New York: Teachers College Press, 1995.

Higgins, Chris. *The Good Life of Teaching: An Ethics of Professional Practice*. Malden, MA: John Wiley & Sons, 2011.

Holt, John. *How Children Learn: 50th Anniversary Edition*. New York: Hachette Book Group, 2017 (1967).

hooks, bell. *Teaching to Transgress: Education as the Practice of Freedom*. New York: Routledge, 1994.

Horkeimer, Max. *The Eclipse of Reason*. New York: Bloomsbury Academic, 2013.

Hutchins, Robert M. "Ideals in Education." *The American Journal of Sociology* 43, no. 1 (1937): 1.

Jackson, Philip. *Life in Classrooms*. New York: Teachers College Press, 1990.

Jackson, Phil W. *What Is Education?* Chicago: Chicago University Press, 2012.

James, William. "The Will to Believe." In *William James: Writings 1878–1899: Psychology, Briefer Course / The Will to Believe / Talks to Teachers and Students / Essays.* edited by Gerald E. Myers. New York: Library of America, 1992.

Kahneman, Daniel. *Thinking Fast and Slow*. New York: Farrar, Straus and Giroux, 2011.

Kanna, Elizabeth, Lisa Gills, and Christina Culver. *Virtual Schooling: A Guide to Optimizing Your Child's Education*. New York: St. Martin's Press, 2009.

Kieran, Egan. *The Future of Education: Reimagining Our Schools from the Ground Up*. New Haven: Yale university Press, 2010.

Koretz, Daniel. *Measuring Up: What Educational Testing Really Tell Us?* Cambridge: Harvard University Press, 2009.

Lemov, Doug. *Teach Like a Champion 2.0: 62 Techniques that Put Students on the Path to College*. San Francisco: Jossey-Bass, 2015.

Lincoln, Bruce. *Authority*. Chicago, University of Chicago Press, 1994.

MacIntyre, Alasdair. *After Virtue*. 3rd edn. South Bend: University of Notre Dame, 2010.

Martin, Jane Roland. "Two Dogmas of Curriculum." *Synthese* 51, no. 1 (Apr., 1982): 5–20.

Marx, Karl. "Theses on Feuerbach." In *The German Ideology*. New York: Prometheus Books, 1998.

McClintock, Robbie. *Homeless in the House of Intellect: Formative Justice and Education as an Academic Study*. New York: Laboratory for Liberal Learning, 2005.

Merleau-Ponty, Maurice. *Phenomenology of Perception*, trans. Donald A. Landes, 2nd edn. New York: Routledge Classics, 2002.

Metro-Roland, Dini and Paul Farber. "The Eclipse of Civic Virtue: Recalling the Place of Public Education." In *Philosophy of Education 2012*, edited by Claudia Ruitenberg. Urbana: The Philosophy of Education Society, 2012.

Metro-Roland, Dini. "Hip Hop Hermeneutics and Multicultural Education: A Theory of Cross-Cultural Understanding." *Educational Studies* 46, no. 6 (2010): 560–78.

Metro-Roland, Dini. "Knowledge, Power, and Care of the Self." In *Beyond Critique: Exploring Critical Social Theories and Education*, edited by Barry Levinson et al. New York, Paradigm Publishers, 2011.

Miron, Gary, Christopher Shank, and Caryn Davidson. "Report Full-time Virtual and Blended Schools: Enrollment, Student Characteristics, and Performance." National Education Policy Center. Boulder, CO: National Education Policy Center, May 2018.

Moe, Terry and John Chubb. *Liberating Learning: Technology, Politics and the Future of American Education*. San Francisco: Jossey-Bass, 2009.

Murdoch, Iris. *The Sandcastle*. New York: Penguin Press, 1978.

Murdoch, Iris. *Sovereignty of Good*. Boston: Ark Paperbooks, 1970.

Neill, Alexander S. *Summerhill School: A New View of Childhood*. New York: St. Martin's Press, 1992 (1962).

Noddings, Nel. *Caring: A Relational Approach to Ethics and Moral Education*. Los Angeles: California, 2013 (1984).

Nussbaum, Martha. *Cultivating Humanity: A Classical Defense of Reform in Liberal Education*. Cambridge: Harvard University Press, 1998.

Oakeshott, Michael. *The Voice of Liberal Learning*. Indianapolis: Liberty Fund, 2001.

Oliver, Mary. "Wild Geese." In *New and Selected Poems*: Vol. 1. Boston: Beacon Press, 1992.

"Our Purpose." *Geelong Grammar School*. Accessed April 7, 2019. https://www.ggs.vic.edu.au/School/Our-School/our-purpose

Palloff, Rena M. and Keith Pratt. *Building Online Learning Communities: Effective Strategies for the Virtual Classroom*, 2nd edn. San Francisco: Jossey-Bass, 2007.

Paris, Django and H. Samy Alim, eds. *Culturally Sustaining Pedagogies: Teaching and Learning for Justice in a Changing World*. New York: Teachers College Press, 2017.

Plato. *The Republic of Plato*. trans. James Adam. Cambridge: Cambridge University Press, 1902.

Ravitch, Diane. *Reign of Error: The Hoax of the Privatization Movement and the Danger to America's Public Schools*. New York: Random House, 2013.

Ricoeur, Paul. *Interpretation Theory: Discourse and the Surplus of Meaning*. Fort Worth: Texas Christian University Press, 1976.

Rizga, Kristina. *Mission High: One School, How Experts Tried to Fail It, and the Students and Teachers who made it Triumph*. New York: Nation Books, 2015.

Shakespeare, William. "That Time of Year Thou Mayst in Me Behold" (Sonnet 73). In *Arden Shakespeare Complete Works*. London: Thomson Learning, 2001.

Sidorkin, Alexander. "Is Schooling a Consumer Good? A Case against School Choice But Not the One You Had in Mind." In *Philosophy of Education 2007*, edited by Nicholas Burbules. Urbana: Philosophy of Education Society, 2007.

Sizer, Theodore R. and Nancy Faust Sizer. *The Students Are Watching*. Boston: Beacon Press, 1999.

Snyder, Rick. *Special Message from Governor Rick Snyder: Educational Reform.* Lansing, MI: Michigan Legislature, April 27, 2011.

Spark, Muriel. *The Prime of Miss Jean Brodie.* New York: Harper Perennial, 1962.

Steffe, Leslie P. and Jerry Gale, eds. *Constructivism in Education.* New York: Routledge Press, 2009 (1995).

Stengel, Barbara S. and Alan R. Tom. *Moral Matters: Five Ways to Develop the Moral Life of Schools.* New York: Teachers College Press, 2006.

Strawson, P. F. "Freedom and Resentment." In *Freedom and Resentment, and Other Essays.* New York: Routledge, 2015 (1974).

Suddendorf, Thomas. *The Gap: The Science of What Separates Us from Other Animals.* New York: Basic Books, 2013.

Taylor, Charles. *The Language Animal: The Full Shape of the Human Linguistic Capacity.* Cambridge: Harvard University Press, 2016.

Toyama, Kentaro. *Geek Heresy: Rescuing Social Change from the Cult of Technology.* New York: PublicAffairs, 2015.

Tuan, Yi-Fu. *Space and Place.* Minneapolis: University of Minnesota Press, 1977.

Tyack, David and Larry Cuban. *Tinkering Toward Utopia: A Century of Public School Reform.* Cambridge: Harvard University Press, 1995.

Tyler, Ralph. *Basic Principles of Curriculum and Instruction.* Chicago: University of Chicago Press, 2013 (1949).

Tyson, Lois. *Critical Theory Today: A User-Friendly Guide.* New York: Routledge Press, 2015.

"Vision and Mission." *Eton School.* Accessed April 7, 2019. https://www.eto nschool.org/about/visionmission

"Vision and Mission." *Upper Canada College.* Accessed April 7, 2019. https://www.ucc.on.ca/welcome/vision-and-mission

Wallace, David Foster. "Authority and American Usage." In *The David Foster Wallace Reader.* New York: Little, Brown and Company, 2014.

Wallace, David Foster. "2005 Kenyon Commencement Address." Accessed March 9, 2019. https://web.ics.purdue.edu/~drkelly/DFWKenyonAddre ss2005.pdf

"What Makes Greenhills Exceptional." *Greenhills School.* Accessed April 7, 2019. https://www.greenhillsschool.org/about/our-purpose/

Whitehead, Alfred North. *The Aims of Education.* New York: Free Press, 1957 (1929).

Williams, James. *Stand Out of Our Light: Freedom and Resistance in the Attention Economy*. New York: Cambridge University Press, 2018

Williams, John. *Stoner*. New York: New York Review Book, 2003 (1965).

Wolff, Tobias. *This Boy's Life*. New York: Grove Press, 1989.

Woodruff, Paul. *Reverence: Renewing a Forgotten Virtue*. New York: Oxford University Press, 2001.

Young, Michael. *The Rise of the Meritocracy*. 2nd edn. New York: Transaction Publishers, 1994.

Index